"... a classic of its kind – every new college teacher should know it ... It tells us what we can and must do in the way of loving and cherishing student creativity ... *the* way to the best education, a mutual enjoyment passionately shared by teacher and student."

JOHN ASHMEAD, Haverford College

"... a personable and compassionate rap ... One of the best things about it is the candid way Macrorie talks about the contempt that underlies academic relations ... and the teaching mistakes to which that contempt testifies."

Big Rock·Candy Mountain

"... a splendid new book about the teaching of English and particularly writing ... It has some superb writing by students."

JOHN HOLT, What Do I Do Monday

"... one of those rare teachers who have the magic of being able to help students discover themselves and write better in the process."

FRANK McLAUGHLIN, Media & Methods

Uptaught

by

KEN MACRORIE

Western Michigan University

HAYDEN BOOK COMPANY INC., NEW YORK

ACKNOWLEDGMENTS

Short passages and examples in this book have previously appeared in *The Western Review* and *Unduressed,* publications of student writing at Western Michigan University, and in publications of the author: an article "To Be Read" in *The English Journal,* May, 1968; a review of *The Analysis of Essays by Computer* in *Research in the Teaching of English,* fall, 1969; an article in *The Michigan English Teacher,* October-November, 1969; a high-school text, *Writing To Be Read,* and a college text, *Telling Writing.*

The passages from *A Writer Teaches Writing* by Donald M. Murray (Houghton Mifflin, Boston, 1968) are reprinted by permission of the publisher, as are the short excerpts from Gerald Levin and Francis Connolly's *A Rhetoric Case Book* (Harcourt, Brace & World, New York, 1969).

For S. William Cook,
who believed in this book.

 Library of Congress Catalog Card Number 70-115961.
Printed in the United States of America

7 8 9 PRINTING

74 75 76 77 78 YEAR

*I know a professor at Western who was talking to a class of 250 students on "Openness" with his fly unzipped.**

PC

CONTENTS

Prologue, 2

PERCIVAL, 3

ENGFISH, 9

FREEDOM, 19

DISCIPLINE, 25

EXAMINATION, 45

TESTIMONY, 53

SLAVERY, 59

OVERSEERS, 77

GRADES, 89

QUESTIONS, 97

PERFORMANCE, 111

PERSONS, 129

GRADUATE SCHOOL, 135

UNDERGRADUATE DAYS, 145

DESPAIR, 149

HOPE, 157

THE THIRD WAY, 167

*The passages in this book printed in italics were written or spoken by students.

PROLOGUE

At 10:48 p.m., April 3, 1969, I watched the president of my university leave his mansion and, followed by about thirty white-helmeted policemen carrying clubs and marching in tight formation behind him, stride across the street and up the walk of the Student Union to clear out any students who insisted on sitting in the Snack Bar after the eleven o'clock closing hour.

I had been a professor more than twenty years. The sight was new, and it made me sick.

Not because the president was acting irrationally.

Not because the students were acting irrationally.

But because the professors were not there. In the last five years I had learned something about their responsibility in this affair. More than anyone else, they have made the university sick unto death.

Yet I have chosen to remain at this school. I think it a first-rate institution of higher learning when compared to others in the country. First-rate, and not very good.

My colleagues treat me well and I like most of them. They seem above the run of professors I have known elsewhere—fair and decent men and women remarkably lacking in arrogance and pretension. The president and the deans I know well. They are usually friendly and supportive. They give us professors almost unlimited freedom of action.

But neither the administrators nor the police nor the students have the power to change what is deeply wrong with this university, with all American colleges and universities. They can bloody each other's heads forever and not improve what happens in the classroom, where the action really is.

There the professors are failing, every day, every hour. This book is the story of how I came to that knowledge.

This way of keeping young persons
in line, of making sure
they do not speak in their own voices
of anything that counts for them,
goes back to Roman times
when schoolboys declaimed on
proper topics in weekly themes. It
is an ancient tradition,
one of the principal causes of whining
boys crawling like snails
unwillingly to school.

PERCIVAL

I received a letter from the editor of the journal *Research in the Teaching of English* asking me to review a report called *The Analysis of Essays by Computer* written by two men at the University of Connecticut at Storrs and published by the United States Department of Health, Education, and Welfare.

The report arrived bulking large as the *Spring through Summer Sears Roebuck Catalog*. The purpose of the study was to find out if computers could analyze and evaluate students' essays as well as teachers do. Six years ago, before my eyes were opened to what professors do in classrooms, I would have admired that purpose. Every English teacher from grade school through graduate school has wanted such a device, because grading themes desiccates the mind.

I found the two researchers had proceeded with care, ingenuity, and liberal spirit. They showed themselves dedicated to finding truth rather than pleasing answers. They looked at the writing of more than 250 high school students—four essays from each—and had the themes punched into the computer so they were part of its memory bank. They figured out what was measurable by the machine that would help it rate the student papers on ideas or content, organization, style, mechanics, and creativity. Then they asked the computer to do its thing.

The men who thought the computer might be able to grade a theme as well as an English teacher did were right.

It could. It did.

They figured the theme graded high by a teacher would carry a large number of these characteristics: a variety of sentence structures, frequent long sentences (with dependent clauses and other clearly realized relationships), a title (many papers did not carry titles), frequent paragraphing, few apostrophes, few spelling errors, many connective words, many commas and parentheses marks. The computer could read the papers for these mechanical traits.

The researchers knew English teachers, all right. They set up their computer to act like one.

My first reaction was that the computer was being terribly limited in its reading. But then I remembered that the researchers intended it to evaluate the "creativity" of the themes, and for a second I began to admire anyone who could sense the relationship of such a barren mark as a parenthesis to the curve of a mind making distinctions. And I liked the description of what would constitute a high degree of creativity: ". . . new and fruitful way of looking at the problem . . . new data in treating the topic . . . a fresh and interesting way of using language. . ."

I thought if the computer was programmed to look for creative writing—no matter by what means, even counting commas—there must be some lively papers among the thousand that it had been turned on to. But as I looked through the 269-page report, I found no papers reproduced, live or dead. I found lists of hundreds of words (the basic vocabulary the computer could read and react to), lists of parenthetical expressions, clichés, etc. But no words that combined to say anything, so I might judge the vigor of thought or expression.

On page 173 I finally found one sentence from a theme: "Money becomes a hindrance when it ceases to aid in the attainment of one of the best things and becomes a goal itself." A nice thought. Old. Tired. Expressed with flattening impersonality and abstractness. Nobody would dare say anything else along that line about money except perhaps Howard Hughes.

I kept looking through that report for some writing that could be said to have been created. Maybe there were a few other sentences I missed. All I found beyond the researchers' description of what they had done (and I must say their language was clear and unpedantic) were sample pages of what the computer typed out. Remarks like this:

S1 (4) CHAR (1) INITIAL ('A', 'A', 'B', 'B'), /° AABB°/

Necessary stuff, I realize, to explain how the computer was used. And I mean *used;* for all of a sudden I found myself thinking of the computer as a person, like Hal in the movie *2001: A Space Odyssey.* When I came to Chapter VIII, I could not do otherwise for there I found the computer writing notes to the student.

If the student writes "busted" the compucer responds, "Do you really think the past participle of 'break' is 'busted' or were you just being careless?"

This note-writer had to have a name. I christened him *Percival.*

Poor Percival—told to look for a "fresh and interesting way of using language," he found himself telling the student he couldn't use the word *busted.* Like an English teacher he was teaching himself and his student to be dry and dead with the English language, that instrument the teacher said possessed such rich and varied resources.

The fact is that *busted* belongs to the pressing, dramatic world of the campus today. Those students who planned to upset the administrators of my university by sitting in the Snack Bar in the Student Union were inviting being busted by the cops, and that's what happened to them. In actuality they had sat in on a Tuesday and got away with it. The president and the cops anticipated they would do the same on Thursday and busted them. The word has a hard and particular meaning at the moment; and any computer or teacher who would deny its use to students writing themes is bound to get papers that are mechanical exercises which carefully avoid telling truths about the world the writers live in.

Percival could be taught to analyze and rate a thousand student themes as well as a teacher because the themes were probably all dead. I mean *dead,* so no one could say even, "This theme moves a little more than that one." The task given to Percival is the same that English teachers have been bitching about for decades, centuries.

In 1756 the British dramatist Colley Cibber wrote, "I remember I was once whipp'd for my theme." Writing those damned and damning things in English-speaking schools has been an insulated act which produced writing no one except a schoolmaster ever read, and he only if forced and paid.

Percival incarnate is a monster who helps us see the English teacher incarnate—a cultivated, liberal, well-intentioned pusher of the life of the mind and feelings, dedicated to promoting moving and memorable expressions of the complexities of life. With his bloody marks in the margins of themes. With his refined and polite comments, like this one by Percival:

> Well, Johnny H. Doe, it was nice to talk to you and to read your essay.

It was not nice to look at Johnny's carefully prepared dead body of a theme, cleaned of all the dirt of the street and the lines of experience around the eyes, inflated with abstract pedantic words, depersonalized with pseudo-objective phrases that rendered it like every other corpse submitted to teacher.

Percival had carried out a monstrous act for his masters, asking Johnny to say something so valuable on paper that it was worth study and care and criticism, and yet depriving him of a true voice in which to say it.

It is proper that the creators of Percival were college men Because it is the university which sets the false tone of American writing, not the grade-school teacher or the businessmen. While asking for "direct and vigorous expression," the English professor has dehumanized the writing of his students. Busted their tongues. And taught himself to write so dully that few of his colleagues can stand to read his articles in learned journals even in their own fields. He writes textbooks that begin like this:

> If you are a student who desires assistance in order to write effectively and fluently, then this textbook is written for you.

That language has no tongue in it. No ear behind it. And no sense of audience. The student instantly perceives that the expression "who desires assistance in order to write effectively and fluently" is walking on stilts. And so he learns the style. Must be what the professor wants. And the grade-school and high-school teacher are among the students of the professor in graduate school. They go back to their pupils with a clear idea of what is needed to prepare youngsters for the higher education.

In the university the base of the whole academic endeavor has traditionally been the Freshman Composition course, where the student learns to write. Not to write truths that count for him. Not to connect his experience to what he reads and hears about in the classroom, but to master an academic tongue and a manner of footnoting and snipping out other persons' words and rearranging them in a new introduction-body-conclusion form. "Tell 'em what you're gonna tell 'em, tell 'em, and then tell 'em what you told 'em." And that will finish them off. Make sure they will look at your paper to see how many pages it takes up rather than what it says.

This dehydrated manner of producing writing that is never read is the contribution of the English teacher to the total university.

I know. For seventeen years I talked and responded like Percival. Then something happened in my class that showed me I had been an automaton sending out subtle messages I was unaware of. The students read them well: they were to become automatons too.

Finding out what I, and other English professors, have been up to all these years has at the same time revealed to me the blindness of all university professors in all fields.

I have written retrospectively a journal of my dark night and awakening. The earliest entry in that record follows.

A language in which fresh truth
is almost impossible to express.

Engfish

(September, 1947)

My students were alive

The students in the first class I ever taught were World War II veterans. The room was never filled, usually a half dozen or so absentees, who I feared were wandering around Chapel Hill enjoying themselves. One day I ran into one of them on campus ten minutes after my class. He walked alongside unabashed, talking of the weather, then said, "*I hope you'll excuse my absences. I like the class, but I flew fighter planes in combat and still get the shakes. Every once in a while I have to bust loose. Usually I jump on a bus and ride anywhere for a few days.*"

(October, 1947)

And humorous

Two weeks later, I opened the classroom door—every seat occupied. Place looked bursting. I assumed mock surprise and said, "There must be some mistake. Do you realize this is English 1, the University of North Carolina, Chapel Hill, North Carolina?"

From the back row hurried and loud, came the words, "Oh, *North* Carolina! '

A book cover popped shut, and a young man rushed out the door and slammed it. When the laughter subsided, he came back in and returned to his seat, wearing his triumph modestly.

(January, 1948)

BUT THEY WROTE DEAD

Like this:

I found the characters in this story very interesting. The plot was exciting and an outstanding aspect of the story was its description.

Except for one boy, McDonald. After writing a few miserable, pretentious, academic papers, he went away for a while. He returned with a paper written in red ink. On the last page the words became indistinguishable, the letters more and more uncertain until they finally squiggled off in a wavy line. I was incensed. The red was so hard to read, and the carelessness insulting.

But as I puzzled out the paper, I found McDonald had produced a zany story of his adventures as exciting and humorous as Holden Caulfield's. Twice more McDonald turned in live, squirming papers. After the final exam he took me aside and explained he had written those papers while he was drunk.

I should have realized that a cataclysmic event was needed to break a student away from the dead language of the schools—some severe displacement or removal from the unreal world of the university, like drunkenness. But I didn't. I was beginning my teaching, and, naturally enough, developing a protective blindness.

(February, 1948)

MY EGO WAS BEING FULFILLED

I had a captive audience but thought I was freeing their minds. Surely they were learning great things from me. I was only a part-time instructor but felt the weight of the trappings of academic prestige and rank. When I walked through the campus carrying my briefcase—an object few students owned in those days—or authoritatively removed a drawer from the card catalog in the library to look up a book, I imagined all the students were looking at me and saying with awe, "He's an instructor."

But the troops weren't performing their job, which was to write clearly and powerfully in my classes. I thought that was their fault.

(March, 1948)

WHAT TEACHER WANTED

In the columns of *The Daily Tarheel,* the student newspaper appeared many swinging, ironic letters to the editor written by undergraduates. They carried the rhythms of human voices, the tension of anger, the dry sound of understatement. Good models of writing for my freshmen.

I tried to get my students to write like that—as if they were on fire about something—but they kept turning out phony paragraphs. Like blacks who know the white man's attitude toward them better than he does himself, they knew what Teacher really wanted, although I didn't. And they gave it to me.

(September, 1948)

I LEARNED HOW TO CORRECT PAPERS, NOT READ THEM

Got a job at Michigan State and settled down to full-time teaching. I bought some red ink for my fountain pen and began writing in the margins of what we called *themes*—

too gen'l
awk
punct
agr
sp
need specific examples

One day I climbed on the table in the classroom and took a beseeching attitude. "Won't you please put down something specific in your next theme?"

No, students turned in empty paragraphs like this:

I went downtown for the first time. When I got there I was completely astonished by the hustle and the bustle that was going on. My first impression of the downtown area was quite impressive.

(October, 1948)

I SAID, "THEY CAN'T WRITE THIS DEAD."

A colleague showed me a book by a University of Minnesota professor designed to cure students who "bandy about vague uninteresting generalizations with no specific examples to back them up."

Off to the Snack Bar with my students to follow the man's prescription—make a chart for the Observation and Recording of Sensory Detail . Columns for (1) Form or Outline, (2) Motion or Position, (3) Shade or Color. Shorter columns for Sound, Smell, Touch, and Taste. Now fill the columns, combine words or phrases into sentences, construct paragraphs. Choose an Overall Impression.

In they came—papers full of bland, trite phrases like those the Minnesota man said were "by and large successful"—

Spreading elm tree,
huge gray skyscrapers,
huge gray glacial rocks. . .

I had forced the arms, guided the fingers—to a huge gray result.

(September, 1951)

I TRIED EVERYTHING, INCLUDING NON-DIRECTION

I would get those kids to write live. Tried general semantics, logic, tape-recorded conversations, ancient rhetoric.

Nothing worked.

I flipped all the way over from the Snack Bar guided exercises to Group Dynamics non-directed style. Got permission to teach sort of Carl Rogers' way. I sat in the back of the room, talked only about five or ten minutes of the fifty, and asked the students to run the class. They chose what to write on, decided what they thought was good writing, and graded each other's papers.

Grading bugged them. At first they wanted to give everyone A and I said no. Slipped a little into direction there. Then they discovered that spelling and other mechanics would give them a standard, and almost all the grades went down to C.

In the first weeks they didn't believe I was going to let them run the class. Halfway through the course many began to enjoy their freedom.

But nobody wrote live. Same old academic stuff—no conviction, no redblooded sentences.

(June, 1957)

I BEGAN WRITING A TEXTBOOK

I tried to play down grammar and mechanics and get the students to write naturally of things that interested them. This book was going to reform the teaching of writing in America.

One thing wrong—it carried no extended examples of good student writing. But I didn't see the implications of that fact. If I could not provide a bunch of lively papers written by students using the program I espoused in my book, then I had nothing to give students and teachers substantially different from what they had been given before.

The book was published by a reputable house—Harcourt, Brace. Its editors insisted I call it *The Perceptive Writer, Reader, and Speaker*. Good title for a book by an author absolutely blind to what he was doing.

(September 1960)

SAN FRANCISCO STATE

In 1960 I left Michigan State for San Francisco State, a school then rated among the top four in the country for teaching creative writing. Although I was hired as a "communication expert" rather than a man who would teach the writing of novels, short stories, and poems, I thought the atmosphere by the beautiful bridge probably made students flower into writers even in composition courses.

I expected exotic real flowers in Golden Gate Park and found them. I expected sophisticated students (the year before many at State and Berkeley had had their backbones bounced against the hard edges of the steps of City Hall by the police in the most publicized student rebellion up to that time) and literary artists as colleagues. I found only the latter. I joined a staff of teachers that included Walter Van Tilburg Clark (he was on leave but his influence was manifest), Mark Harris, Harvey Swados, and S. I. Hayakawa.

Indeed it was a writing place, and most of the professors I knew were three times as alive as most I had known at Michigan State. Caroline Shrodes, who had collected all the exciting writers, enchanted me. I had never before met a woman head of a department, and no professor who one day wore giant-sized blue earrings with high-heeled shoes to match, and the next day the same combination in shocking pink. She tapped her foot with a nervous energy that seemed to vibrate through that department, and I knew I had found the right place.

It was a wonder. Caroline told me that to teach one especially small class of students weak in writing, I would be given an assistant. I expected a pale, ineffectual boy and got a bright, deeply sensitive young woman who had just given up her job as the office boss for Kermit Bloomgarden on Broadway, where she helped him with the production of *The Music Man*. I began the semester with the highest of hopes.

The papers my students turned in were worse, if anything, than those I had received at Michigan State. I was down on my knees again pleading for sentences partially alive.

After a year, I left San Francisco State. I had met stimulating professors there, but not stimulating students. The city was dramatic and beautifully situated, as well as dirty in the Mission District and Walt Disneyish in the suburbs. I missed the white winters and green springs of Michigan; so I returned there to take a job in an unlikely sounding place called Kalamazoo.

(February, 1962)

I BECAME A LEADER OF COMPOSITION TEACHERS

I was appointed editor of *College Composition and Communication*, a journal published by the National Council of Teachers of English. In that job I read and edited hundreds of plans for saving the dying composition course.

I was determined to publish some bright student writing to show readers their students weren't hopeless. I looked hard for it, solicited the 3,500 teachers who subscribed to the journal, and turned up about three decent papers. I printed them and got this letter from a professor in Ohio:

Why a new "arty" cover; and especially why undergraduate writing? . . . Why pretend that we are all undergraduates and want to read about each other's first impressions of college?

After that, I began to notice hundreds of signs suggesting that most English professors despised their students' work. They should have. It was usually terrible.

(February, 1963)

SIXTEEN YEARS NOW TEACHING BLIND

I had devoted most of my career to teaching Freshman Composition because I wanted every college student to write with clarity and pezazz. Sometimes attending my class, students became worse writers, their sentences infected with more and more phoniness, and eventually stiffening in *rigor mortis*. One of my freshmen at Western Michigan University turned in this paragraph:

I consider experience to be an important part in the process of learning. For example, in the case of an athlete, experience plays an important role. After each game, he tends to acquire more knowledge and proficiency, thereby making him a better athlete. An athlete could also gain more knowledge by studying up on the sport, but it is doubtful he could participate for the first time in sports with study alone and without experience and still do an adequate job.

Such language could only have been learned in school; no one anywhere else would hear it in the bones of his ear. Key university words are there: *process, experience, role, tend, knowledge, proficiency, participate,* and *important* twice. But nothing is said worth listening to. I thought this paragraph acceptable—medium rotten, but all I could expect.

(October, 1963)

MAYBE OUTSIDE OF CLASS?

Maybe they're afraid to say what they feel. Maybe the assignments are too confining.

With the help of other professors in a communication program, I arranged a contest—$150 for the best essay on any subject touching university life, $150 to the judge of the contest. To encourage students to speak out, I asked Paul Goodman, author of *Growing Up Absurd*, to judge the essays. In a university then comprised of 11,000 students, we received eight essays in the competition. All dead. None seemed stirring enough to warrant a certification of life, much less a prize. But I sent them off to Mr. Goodman. He read them and wrote back:

> This isn't a very spirited group of essays, and I cannot award a prize to any. Nothing sends me—neither original idea, acute observation, accurate analysis, unique attitude, warm feeling, nor vivid expression. There is no sense in making a comparative judgment among the pieces. . .
> My impression is that the young people have been so brainwashed by their social background and their so-called education that even their dissent is stereotyped, griping rather than radical, snobbish rather than indignant, do-goodish rather than compassionate. There is little sign of careful, painful perception, personal suffering, or felt loyalty and disgust. On the other hand, the couple of positive estimates of university experiences are not ideal, or loving, enough to be moving. . .

(November, 1963)

NO NEED TO EXAMINE THE BODY

Paul Goodman was right. And the incontrovertible fact was that back in 1960 the profession had become so sick of spending more money and time on the Freshman Comp course than any other that the head of the English Department of the University of Michigan, Warner Rice, proposed in a lead article in *College English* that the freshman writing course be abolished because it wasn't producing competent writing from students.

Mr. Rice wasn't kidding; he s not a kidding man. Many professors who had given their lives to this effort felt insulted, but I didn't hear of one who came forward with a batch of lively student papers to prove Mr. Rice wrong.

(December, 1963)

A NAME FOR IT

A student stopped me in the hall and said, "*Do you think I should submit this to* The Review? *I have this terrible instructor who says I can't write. Therefore I shouldn't teach English. He really grinds me.*"

I looked at the first two lines:

He finks it humorous to act like the Grape God Almighty, only the stridents in his glass lisdyke him immersely.

and thought they seemed like overdone James Joyce. I said I had better take the paper home and give it several readings before reacting. But she pushed, and I read the next lines,

Day each that we tumble into the glass he sez to mee, "Eets too badly that you someday fright preach Engfish."

I wanted to hug that girl. She had been studying Joyce in another class and had used his tongue to indict all of us Engfish teachers. Didn't believe I had lisdyked my students all those years, but I had indeed tumbled them into a glass every day and fright preached Engfish at them. This girl had given me a name for the bloated, pretentious language I saw everywhere around me, in the students' themes, in the textbooks on writing, in the professors' and administrators' communications to each other. A feel-nothing, say-nothing language, dead like Latin, devoid of the rhythms of contemporary speech A dialect in which words are almost never "attached to things," as Emerson said they should be.

All those years I thought students needed to be forced. Because I was always telling them, they had no chance to tell me.

Freedom

(May 5, 1964)

Freedom

The winter had been dark and spirits down. I said I could no longer face another student paper written in Engfish. I told my Advanced Writing class, "Go home and write anything that comes to your mind. Don't stop. Write for ten minutes or till you've filled a whole page." I had remembered reading about that exercise in Dorothea Brande's book *Becoming a Writer,* published in 1936, and I had used the exercise briefly with students in Chapel Hill. My advanced writers returned with papers that spoke disjointedly and fragmentarily, but in language often alive. Some natural rhythms appeared, a striking metaphor once in a while, and often a bit of reality that jarred me. Karen Feldkamp turned in this:

Bought a red ball.

Therapy. But it doesn't work. The hair on my legs still keeps growing. Sensuously round clouds, standing at attention, waiting in rows for inspection. Made me feel happy and light, young. Nature does that to me. Makes me fresh and alive. Never smoke when I'm in the woods or by a lake. It would tarnish the beauty. I want money. I want to feel rich so that I can know what nothing is like. Makes me think of Gibran. He says sorrow and joy are relative. Must know sorrow to know joy. I believe in him. I believed in a lot of things once.

I've decided to advise people on the subject of love. World don't close your eyes when you kiss. I hope someone hears me. I've seen too many made rancid and disposed of. I wish I could act as I think. My mind knows, but my body doesn't. Does it? Some girls in Detroit attacked a girl in an alley, pierced her cheeks and legs with safety pins. I don't know why it made me laugh so hard. My breath smells. Must be from that milk. People think milk is so good for them. It's bad for their complexion, fattening, and causes hardening of the arteries. You're no damn good when your arteries get hard.

(May 7, 1964)

THE DAY WE KILLED ENGFISH

Then I asked the students to do another free writing, this time for fifteen minutes focusing on one subject. The day we met to read those papers was hot, so we went outside under a tall maple on heavy grass still new in Michigan's spring. Twelve out of the fourteen students were present, friendly and pleasant as usual, looking around abstractedly, probably hoping the Engfish they were about to hear would quickly dissipate in the outside air.

I asked the girl nearest me to read her paper. She had written about working at an ambulance service where one day she heard the doorbell ringing as if someone were leaning on it. I thought here we go with the cliche and the standard tired paper. But as she read on, I found that a person had indeed been leaning on the bell, "*a chartreuse-faced woman choking out that her husband was having a heart attack.*"

That paper by Julie Oldt Maxson moved me. Not until I heard the third paper that afternoon did I realize that everyone on the grass had quit gazing around and was listening hard. Each student had written a powerful short paper and I had broken through and the students were speaking in their own voices about things that counted for them.

(May 11, 1964)

Progress?

Immediately I tried the same free writing in Freshman Comp and got almost as good papers. One boy who was flunking the course writing broken sentences and spelling incomprehensibly, turned in a strong account of driving home after a party. His spelling was much improved and he controlled his words. He built to the skillful rhythms of this ending:

Then out of the fog loomed a red sign—STOP. The end of the road. I had miscounted. Sign, trees, ditch, fog, brakes, beer, that's all I remembered.

A whole semester passed before I realized I should *begin* my classes with free writing. After that, they were writing complete stories in the second and third week. Their papers exhibited all the qualities Paul Goodman said were lacking in the essays he judged. The writers revealed a surprising occasional command of metaphor, forceful beginnings and endings, telling detail, word play, irony. All those years I had tried to get a student to put down a sensuous detail that would bring alive his ideas and feelings! Now I simply ask students to write freely, first recording random thoughts, then focusing on one subject, and they frequently produce what the poet Wallace Stevens called "the exquisite environment of fact."

(May, 1965)

"Recording Sensory Details"

In twenty minutes of free writing, a freshman girl produced this paper:

In a few minutes Mom and Dad are going out to eat. She's got on a long-sleeved yellow dress, black fish-net nylons and black heels. When she doesn't notice, Dad looks at her. Then he rests his head on the back of the red chair and closes his eyes.

Last night Bob brought me home at twelve o'clock. We had been wrestling and playing tag on the grass in the back of Sangren. We were still laughing when he let me out of the car. I pinched his buns and then he messed up my hair. We gave each other a noisy kiss under our five-watt porch light, and he left.

Mom and Dad were still up. I was relieved because I thought we might have wakened them. I started to go upstairs when Dad asked me to wait. I put my books down and sat at the desk. Mom's face was tight and her freckles were little red spots. Dad kept puffing on his pipe. He began. "Your mother and I have decided to get a divorce But even though I'm leaving, remember you're still my daughter and you always will be."

Then he started to cry. Mom and I were crying too. I ran over and put my arms around him. His tears felt hot on my neck. Then he said, "Go to your mother. She feels bad, too."

He left tonight—to his little apartment on Copper Street. Mom helped him move, and she cried when she saw it. The bedroom is lavender with a purple bedspread. The furniture looks like Antique Barn. A big crack runs up and down the door. When he left, he took a lamp, four glasses, and an ash tray.

The details in that little paper speak the pain and tension in a man going to live without his women. Using no chart or program for recording pertinent details, this writer had found her way.

Miss Parklane would write
three titles on the front board
and then each student
could choose the one he liked,
either "A Moral Decision,"
or "Types of Bells,"
or "Wintertime."
These had to be done in pen
so we would learn to write
without erasing.

DISCIPLINE

(April 12, 1966)

PROFESSIONAL DISCIPLINE

In the freshman class Millie Crandall sat at my right not saying a thing for the first two weeks, a little scared and country looking. When time came to hand in a case-history of some process the student knew well, she presented me with a story of her working day at a nearby hospital and care home. It was laconic and powerful.

The students looked at Millie wondering where she had been all that time. She let a few facts open up that world of loneliness and slidings in and out of reality, and ended the account like this:

The hall was dark. As I walked toward the time clock, I heard a few moans. Someone called out, "I want to go home." I punched the time clock, walked out the door.

Millie could walk out; they couldn't. That was the story—told in such exquisitely painful particulars that three hours after it was printed in a campus publication with an 11,000-copy press run, I received a phone call from the president of the university.

"That story in *The Review* this morning about the patients in the home. Was that written by one of your students?"

"Yes."

"Well, it's a good story, full of feeling, but there's one trouble. All the names in it are real."

"Oh, no!" I said. "I'm sure I told everybody in that class to watch out for real names." My mind raced back. Had I said that to Millie's class? I was sure I had. Maybe she had been absent that day.

"Yes," said the president. "And I just got a call from the director of the home. She's quite agitated. Things are said about the patients, personal things, that could be the basis for a libel suit. I wonder if you could get the editors of the paper and the writer together and drive down there to see the director. Maybe you could calm her down and apologize."

"What gets me is that it's such a compassionate story."

"Yes, it is, but things are said about individuals and about the home that shouldn't be publicized with real names."

He was right. I won't cite examples because the details should not be publicized again. Millie was so deeply embarrassed that I didn't think I'd be able to pull her out. The editors and she and I drove to the home and talked to the director. She was agitated, fearing her patients' personal lives would be spread around the county. But she felt comforted to know we admitted wrong. She said she would take all precautions possible to keep copies of *The Review* from reaching the patients. Neither she nor any of them pressed charges against the university. Millie said she could not return to our university next fall, but I insisted she had written a compassionate if searing report on the human condition and we needed students like her. I showed her a letter in which the president said we must not let her turn away from our university for what was only a human mistake.

She came back in the fall, joined the staff of *The Review*, and contributed good writing to it.

Never before had my students written anything alive and honest enough to be dangerous. I was going to have to treat them as potent.

(April 14, 1966)

SIGHT

I began to see how school is really taught in America, from kindergarten through graduate school.

In the First Way the teacher hands out a package of information and tests to see whether students can remember its content. The package contains no gifts, and the teacher expects none in return.

In the Second Way, the teacher provides complete freedom and no direction at all. That way is apt to produce a few splendid, inventive sand castles that are eventually abandoned on a beach strewn with empty beer cans.

In the Third Way, which I stumbled onto, students operate with freedom and discipline. They are given real choices and encouraged to learn the way of experts.

(January 8, 1968)

A Third Way Class

Once I got the new program formulated, almost every writing class went the same way. Because I have a number of papers on hand from a class that met in the winter of 1968, I will present here a record of its journey to show the Third Way.

This Advanced Writing class met twice a week for two hours. Everyone was present at the first meeting except a student named Malcolm Huey, so I explained the program and we were under way. At the third meeting Malcolm arrived an hour late with his pleasantly relaxed hippy look, sat down without a word. He had no writing to turn in. As I was taking out the roll and the papers from my briefcase, John Bird leaned over and read my notation after his name: "weak start."

"*What's that for?*" he asked belligerently. I was angry at his snooping, but had to tell the truth. I explained that his first two papers seemed to be showing off vocabulary rather than saying anything. He sulked the rest of the hour and I fumed. After class I showed him where he had written, "*The door opened to its capacity*" and I said the word *capacity* carried too much horsepower for that spot. He said he knew it wasn't a good word there, and I felt better, and he added, "*But I liked it.*" Already I had lost the Third Way for him—at the beginning there must never be discouragement, only encouragement or no comment at all.

(January 10, 1968)

Barry Chute

In this class in the first free writing I got three short papers that could stand by themselves, even though the students had been asked only to record whatever they were thinking, not to focus on one subject. A paper by David Ballou delighted the students—a memory of his landlady with the garlic breath and a hatred of the Catholic church. "*Heaven to her would be* The New York Times *Sunday edition filled entirely with the obituary.*"

Another paper carried this memory of childhood by Barry Chute:

When I was a kid I was fat It's no fun to be fat. I used to try to be jolly, but that's hard to do when you don't have a damn thing to be jolly about. How can you laugh after you spill your lunch tray all over the cafeteria floor? Or, even worse, to score the winning point in a tense intramural game at the wrong basket. I couldn't run fast, which left out sports, and wasn't jolly enough to raise myself in the social strata, so I became—I guess it was inevitable—a nothing.

But really it's kind of fun to be nothing. You sit around with your nothing friends and laugh at the cool kids as they try to keep up their image. I didn't have to try, which relieved a lot of pressure, and was content in my nothing world, a never-never land between social life and death. It's easier my way, since I can think about other things that are important to a kid—like grades. Every little kid has to get good grades if he's a nothing, since there's little else to do.

This peace was short-lived, because I started to emerge from my ugly duckling shell, and the cool ones recognized that I had potential. So I became one of the cool kids being laughed at by the nothings. But at least now they applaud when I spill my lunch tray all over the cafeteria floor—the applause makes it cool.

(January 15, 1968)

MALCOLM HUEY

Within another week I had received seven fine short pieces of writing from the class. John Bird's prose remained self-conscious and he and I with each other. On the fourth meeting, Malcolm Huey finally turned in something.

I was in swimming lessons at the YMCA, and the lessons were supposed to be natural progressions, and how was I to know, when after they had said I could do it, they who knew what it's all about, that it wasn't really natural? After so much playing around in the shallows, I faking it, doing what I was told, I was a literalist, they took us down to the deep end and told everyone to dive in and swim, swim along the edge of the pool, makes sense, I could see that, and I could see those from the line in front of me making it, and therefore making it true, who was I to doubt, and on my turn, no fear, now was my natural guaranteed time to swim, and I took a leap of faith into the water, and went down and thought I was swimming because who was I to doubt, and when they pulled me up and asked me why I didn't swim, what could I say, I thought I was, I was kicking my feet and swinging my arms, and my hands were cupped like he told me to do, and when another kid my age was telling me the horrible truth of what happened, how the man had casually held onto the diving board with his hands and picked me up between his knees, I was lost to that guaranteed world that everyone else knew, lost behind embarrassment and shall I say again lost, naked, for I knew no defenses, there were my emotions, and doubts as to everything and terrible scared loneliness. After so many of these things, I began to have doubts towards myself. I just knew it was my fault and I could never keep up. It wasn't until much later in my life that I learned to doubt the givenness of their guaranteed world and began to reassure and relearn myself.

(January 17, 1968)

BIRD STARTS TO FLY

The class sailed along. Slowly John Bird's prose lost its stilted quality and began to pick up colloquial rhythms. In every one of his papers I had looked for words or sentences I could praise. He and I soon realized that he had a keen eye for the way the world goes, even though he often let his vocabulary blur the record of that sight. In about three or four weeks, he broke through with this little paper:

The door opens and this kid bops in. I know him. It's all right, you don't have to knock, just come on in if it's not locked, you know. He flops his body down on the bed and begins scanning a yearbook (Smiling Faces High School) or the latest Playboy *(Sex and the Sophisticated Male). If it's the yearbook, he starts naming off all the ugly girls.*

"Christ, she must be majoring in truckdriving." If it's the Playboy, *it falls open to the foldout (they're designed that way). "She's* O.K., *but I don't like her hips."*

He starts talking about people I know. "You know Linda so and-so, well, she's all screwed up. Well, I know that for a fact, because I hear—" Digging up rumors, second-hand, third-hand, even fourth-hand information, he reworks them into a pseudo-'ogical argument and courtroom oratory.

"I don't care if he's a good friend of yours, he's still an idiot. He's got no ambition. I'd never hire him. Do you know what I heard about him. . ."

Then I just stand up, poke a pencil threateningly in his chest, and push him out the door. I don't talk to him any more. But I still play handball with him.

(January 29, 1968)

A LITTLE DIALOGUE

Halfway through that class, I began my now constant practice of asking students at the outset of the period what was on their minds. One boy frequently would begin speaking before I had the chance to issue the invitation. He almost always said something valuable. When I asked for writing that presented a critical response to a book or other art work, one student told with power and clarity what I thought would be impossible to tell in writing—how he felt listening to electronic music. I had a negative feeling about this miss and perhaps hit kind of music, but hadn't given it much of a chance. His paper opened me to its possibilities. I read it to my wife, who as a teacher of humanities had been playing electronic music to unsympathetic classes. I told the student she wanted his permission to reproduce the paper for her classes. He said he could get a tape recording made of the music as well.

I said my wife needed the tape soon, reminded him twice, tried to call him one evening at the last minute to get the tape, found he had no phone, and set out in my car to track him down. When I located his address, I was told by a man shouting back and forth on a dark street to an unidentified boy that my student had moved. It was getting late for me. I had student papers of my own to read that night. After a confusing trip on strange streets, I found his new address, knocked, and he opened the door surprised in his undershorts. By this time I was edgy.

He said he didn't have the tape but could call his friend and see if he had made it yet. He was piqued because he had to go to another apartment to use another student's phone. I let a little of my irritation show because I thought he should know the difficulty he had caused my wife and me and needed to realize what is required of a teacher who meets his classes responsibly. He didn't lose his temper, but I could tell he was nettled. I jumped in the car, found the next address, and got the tape in time for my wife to use it.

The next time our class met, without a word he handed me an accurate account of my evening's encounter with him, a little play told precisely in every detail, the dialogue absolutely faithful. In his drama, he closed his apartment door after I left and said aloud to himself, "*Fuck you, old man. It wasn't my fault my friend didn't get the recording done on time*"

I wrote on the paper why I had been so angry and we spoke no further of the incident. Later in the semester, he volunteered his services on a project I was working on in the community. I think we both learned from our honest exchange. I had just a touch of the teacher's feeling in thinking anything I asked a student to do should be done with alacrity and gratefulness. He had a touch of the radical student's feeling that anyone who wants to be prompt and responsible is square.

(February 5, 1968)

All-American Girl

One student in that class couldn't take the Engfish off her line. She never located a subject that wanted her. In a paper she described the wonderful summer she had experienced as a counselor at Girls' State, a mock government sponsored every summer by the American Legion on the campus at Michigan State University. She said the girls who were her charges would never forget learning what it is to be an American. The paper elicited no comment from the class. I sat waiting, and finally to fill the void, one student said, "*I don't think you got down to telling what happened at the thing to make you feel it was so successful.*"

"*Yeah,*" said another. "*What does it mean to be an American. You never said. Tell me. It doesn't mean much to me right now.*"

She had nothing to tell him and admitted maybe she hadn't yet found what she wanted to say in the paper. The critics had responded brutally, but I think validly. I talked to the girl after class to encourage her to hunt for truths that had moved her. She thought she knew one, and wrote another paper about her next summer's experience at Girls' State, which she said had been ruined by the hostile attitude of a black girl who had secreted a knife in her room and let the girls know she had it. Here was an experience that had left its impression, but the white girl had not got to know the black girl well enough to make the black girl's hostility seem true. In one or two other papers at the end of the year, this girl improved somewhat, but I failed to move her any significant distance on the Third Way.

She was a rare failure. She had attended the class regularly and gone through the program. I could say she failed because she was stupid and imperceptive, but I rather think she only needed more time. If she had been allowed to take the Third Way for several years in all of her courses, I think her native good sense would have escaped the narrow cabin she had lived in for so many years at home and at school.

(February 7, 1968)

JULIE TEITELBAUM

Mrs. Teitelbaum looked sixteen and I couldn't stop calling her "Miss." She began the course slowly and kept telling me how hard it was for her to open up in writing.

Early in the semester she had turned in a fey paper about a girl friend who left the small town for the big city and returned in a few months without quite knowing why. In telling the story, Julie described how she and her mother had waited at the train station for the adventurer to return, how they had made up games and played them as they sat there. The story was incomplete, not divulging enough about the girl to bring her fully alive, but I couldn't put it out of mind. "I like that girl," I said to Julie. "Why don't you write more about her?"

I mentioned the story twice, and the second time Julie answered, "*You know her.*"

"Who is she?" I asked.

"*She's in this class.*"

I became excited thinking of possibilities. 'Darcy Cudlip?"

"*No.*"

"Well then, I can't guess."

"*She's me* " she said, blushing.

As the weeks passed by, the students and I found Julie continually surprising. When she started to read us the following story in an especially careful, childlike manner, we knew she was setting us up for something.

Alice Dear

She was the prettiest doll I had ever seen, so I gave her the prettiest name I knew, which was Alice. *But that wasn't enough, so I later added* Dear.

One day Mommy took Baby Sister out for a walk in the carriage and I asked if I could take Alice Dear along. So Mommy showed me how to wrap her up like Baby Sister and how to carry her so she would be comfortable, and we went for a walk.

Whenever someone looked at Baby Sister they had to peek under Alice Dear's covers, too. Everyone thought Alice Dear was the prettiest doll they had ever seen, just like they thought Baby Sister was the cutest baby.

I had three dolls, Alice Dear, Patty, and Judy. Patty was a nice doll, but as big as a real baby—much too hard for me to handle. She had a hard plaster head, rubber arms and legs and a cloth body. You couldn't spank Patty very hard because every time you did, she'd always cry back at you—WAH! WAH! I couldn't bear to hear any child of mine cry like that.

Judy was a more grown-up doll. She could walk, but her body was hard and you always had to treat her nice because Mommy said she cost a lot of money.

Alice had an all-rubber body and I could give her a bath every day. She had rooted hair and I could comb it and set it. When I spanked her, she always knew it was for her own good and that it hurt me more than it hurt her. She could take it like a lady. She didn't cry back at me like that ole sissy Patty did.

Alice Dear was cuddly. She was just right in my arms. I could take her to bed with me and if she landed on the floor at night, she didn't mind at all because she knew I loved her. Patty would get mad at me, I know, because Mommy told me once that if she ever landed on the floor her head would break. I couldn't even consider taking Judy to bed with me. Her hard body always poked me and sometimes she'd get stubborn and stick up her leg.

Alice began to wear out from all the baths, and her rubber skin got all black. Though she never grew up like normal children, she got bald from all the times I washed and set her hair.

One hot July day of my ninth year, Alice Dear got a spanking for being naughty. Her soft body couldn't take it any more, and she split right up the back. All her foam rubber stuffing fell out.

I looked at her in surprise. Alice Dear didn't cry, she just gave up. All those shots in her behind from the times we played hospital together, she the patient, I the nurse, stood out like bruises. Suddenly I cried for all the times Alice never did.

I ran in the house and told Mother what happened and she comforted me. Then she took a paper bag and a broom and cleaned up Alice from the garage floor. She saved Alice's head. Alice Dear had a pretty face—rosy cheeks and blue eyes and a dimple that was nice to kiss. I set her head on the window sill in my bedroom for a couple of weeks and then asked Mother about doll factories that take parts from broken dolls and make them into new dolls.

The next day, Daddy took Alice's head away. It was right about that time that I lost interest in dolls.

(February 14, 1968)

DARCY CUDLIP

Darcy was a striking girl with long dark hair, who met everyone without obsequiousness. I liked her because she did not throw her beauty and her experience with men at us as if we should be overwhelmed. I think she was having some personal difficulties, she missed class a number of times, but retained her ability to make the class laugh, as she did with this, her first piece of writing of any length.

First Car

I had driven my first car somewhere between 1,000 and 1,500 miles, and a little slip of white paper in the glove compartment told me it was time for an oil change and grease job. So I pulled into a Shell station and asked if I could make an appointment. I was told to come back two days later at 5:00 and they would have time to do it. On that day I drove in and hauled out that piece of paper that told me what I was supposed to know about keeping my car running.

How many cans of oil does this car hold?' I asked, saying cans *instead of* quarts, pints, *or* gallons, *so I wouldn't seem like I was totally ignorant.*

"It depends on what size can you use." He blew it, but saved me by adding, "It'll hold four of those over there in the window."

I smiled as if to say, "Of course," then like my dad had told me (and written on the piece of paper) I told him how to add the oil.

"OK," I said, "put in one quart less than it will hold and add a can of CD2."

"I never heard of CD2," he retorted. This made me feel superior because here I, just a car-stupid girl, knew about something he didn't.

"How about a can of STP?" he asked. He had to explain that it was an "additive" (which left a big question in my mind, but I kept my mouth shut).

"All right, if you're sure it's the same thing," I answered, knowing he couldn't possibly say it was if he didn't know what CD2 was. "Put in one quart less than it will hold," I repeated, "and add a can of STP."

"Look, little Miss Wisconsin," he boomed—I guess he noticed my license plates—"STP mixes *with the oil. It doesn't increase the oil level."*

"But my dad said—" (I pouted, looking at my little white sheet of salvation). He didn't let me finish.

"That may be true if it's with that other stuff, not with this," he said, shoving a can of STP through the window of the car.

So I relented, figuring he must know more than I did, even if he hadn't ever heard of CD2.

A few days later, I pulled in and a new guy came over to the car.

"Oh, so you're the girl from Wisconsin! What did your dad tell you to do now, put gas in it?"

Right then it became clear that I never could get excited about that car. It never would be mine. It belonged to the garage mechanic, the fuel pump, the oil can, and to the one thing that made it possible to get these—the credit card, which was in my dad's name. Even the charge card belongs to the oil company, really, so I'm just taking that car into its owners to care for, and who am I to tell someone what to do with what belongs to them?

(February 19, 1968)

DAVID BALLOU

Halfway through the course David told me he had been reading a good bit of Hemingway and admired the inter-chapter paragraphs in *In Our Time*. Could he write short stuff like that for a while? Sure, I said. I was committed to letting students depart from assignments if they had good reason to try something else. So David tried it. He achieved the concentration of Hemingway, put the reader there, but only once or twice did the action produce Hemingway's large meanings.

David was starting with the most difficult—ordinarily the wrong way to learn. But he picked up a great deal of discipline. Later he tried longer pieces. I give part of one here, about his friend Bill:

I went to the funeral last month. I saw his mother and said, "Hello," but she didn't reply, just went to the ladies' room and stayed there until I left. Her minister was there; he'd never seen Bill. He introduced himself and asked me, "What was Bill like when you knew him? I mean before he went bad?"

I smiled and said, "He was rotten as hell all the time I knew him." The minister left me alone.

The superintendent of schools was there. In hıgn school he used to pick the sluttiest girls for hall-guards, position them out of sight of the others, and go around each hour furtively attempting to feel them up. Bill and I used to come in a different door every morning and catch him. He finally had to wait until we had arrived to begin servicing the hall-guards. He hated us. He came over and super-smile-handshaked me, asking in his smooth, slimy administrator's voice, "How are you, boy?" He didn't let me answer, but frowned as though preparing to say something of great importance, and went on talking. "Terrible thing, terrible thing to have to happen to his mother. Fine woman, known her since the kids were babies, fine woman. I know them all well. Live just down the street, you know."

I knew.

He continued. "We all thought he'd straightened out when he came home from the army. He looked real good in his uniform. Nice and clean. Neat. But he wouldn't get a job. Just laid around and drank beer and read books. Couldn't talk to him about world affairs, said wild things about the government and the army. He was irrational, wouldn't face reality. Oh, he took to riding a motorcycle too. Fell in with a real bad bunch. I could see that right away—"

I guess he was still talking when I walked outside. I needed a some air. On the way out, I met Bill's younger brother, Bobby. I bought a bottle of wine and some sausage and we walked down to the river. We sat on the bank and talked all afternoon Bobby's in the tenth grade now, same school, people. He said they told him he has an I.Q. of 138, but he was advised to take metal shop, wood shop, typing, physical education, general math, and study hall. He smiled and laughed when he said, "The principal says I'm smart, but I'll never get anywhere because I have a bad attitude "

(February 21, 1968)

MRS. B

With traces of grey in her hair, she was old enough to be the mother of some of the students sitting around the table, and I think she fell in love with David Ballou and several other boys as a mother falls for a son. Her face, one of the most responsive I have seen, showed respect and delight most of the time the young people talked or read their work. She wrote of Wednesdays, when she commuted from a nearby town to the university, fed and advised the family on what to wear, got them off in the morning, delivered her daughter for a music lesson, and returned home to make dinner for a husband who, like most husbands, said, "Well, what did you do today?"

(March 11, 1968)

ALAN APPEL

To encourage the students to write stronger critical pieces, I invited one of my colleagues to talk to the class. He has given *The Saturday Review* and *The New York Times Book Review* some of their few reviews that can stand as literature themselves. He said he had learned to improve his craft by writing 100-word capsule reviews for a library magazine.

I didn't ask the students to try that difficult job, but a week later Alan Appel turned in this little review:

Suffer, Little Children, *by Dr. Max Rafferty, California State Superintendent of Public Instruction—supposedly a collection of essays, actually a circus of classical figures and contradictions.*

Like the Bible, Rafferty's ramblings prove almost anything. "We are teaching trivia." And "to be self-reliant . . . think democratically . . . be decent, kindly, and charitable . . . and . . . love liberty." "Education's first duty is to make possible the survival of our country." ". . . the Slob must go."

School the genius fulltime, for we must face "a race of faceless, godless peasants from the steppes of Asia."

Ten cents of worthwhile material in this sixty-cent Signet book.

(March 13, 1968)

BIRD ON THE WING

In the last month of the semester, John Bird was turning out one strong paper after another. The students were most impressed by his tale of how his childhood friends and he had discovered what they thought was an abandoned privy in the woods, torn it down for fun, only to be accosted by the owner who was still using it.

Then the rebuilding, with John's father understanding the mistake and enjoying the task with the boys. A grand reconstruction of the Roman Empire after the fall.

(March 19,1968)

DAYS

I knew the students in that class, like all those in Third Way classes, only partially. But where I knew them, I knew them deeply. Although our encounters were necessarily less frequent than those one has with a close friend or member of the family, they were almost always marked by an effort to tell truth. In fact, a teacher may admire his students more than members of his family because in the Third Way he knows them mainly at their best, and they do not suffer his forgetting to take out the garbage, his irascible morning temper, or the slings of his scorn for children who fail to hang up their coats.

All but one or two students in that class I know well enough to carry their memory for several years, and a few will never leave me. They were quick and slow, kind and unkind, through the days.

When Martin Luther King, Jr., was assassinated and the talk turned to black-white relations, one boy showed his basic mistrust of blacks as a people. Yet he had written a paper in which he claimed to have discovered a black fellow worker was a better man than he.

About a third of the class had no understanding of why some of the black girls in the dormitory had told their white girl friends they weren't going to speak to them for two weeks after Dr. King's death. They did not see that those two weeks of non-speaking were designed to symbolize two hundred years of whites not speaking to blacks except as servants.

On that day, I was disappointed in six of my students.

(March 28, 1968)

CHUCK BROWN

A few days after the semester had ended, one of my friends in another department stopped me on campus and said, "Ken, my son really got a lot out of that class in writing. Did you know he was my son?"

I was dumbfounded. I had seen the boy years before in his home but in class never connected the name, which was the same as his father's. He sat there at the seminar table speaking and reading his work with such a manly and un-Engfish passion and honesty that he made me cherish his words from the first day on. His father was pleased that I liked his writing, but wanted me especially to say what I thought of the story he had written about a young man who visited his brother in the mental hospital and inadvertently provided the gun that he eventually used to kill himself.

"A good story," I said. "Great feeling."

My friend said, "It's about me. That's my brother in the story, and I provided the means that bought the gun with which he killed himself. I told Chuck the story and he remembered it and got it right in every essential respect. He changed a detail here and there, but he caught all the feelings. I think that's remarkable."

I agreed.

"We thought it would be better if you didn't know Chuck was my son—until he finished his work with you," he said.

A Piece of Plastic

I remember that he was going to be a singer. And I heard his voice and I fought for it to stop. I couldn't help him. After he lost his job —sure enough everyone did at that time, and after his aspirations for being a singer melted and sputtered as madly as grease on a hot skillet and after his kids no longer wanted to hear his stories and after he had stopped listening—he tried to kill himself and I turned the gas off too soon, and after he awoke still alive and lay screaming he wanted to die, I had to beat him unconscious to stop him from trying. And I kept hitting him and he kept trying to get up and Al was holding him from behind and all the time there was this screaming, "I want to die, don't make me live!" and his face was bloody and when I hit him, he splattered on my shirt and then he started to cry and asked me to let him die and all this time my hands kept pounding away until he was still. I held my head in my hands and later when I could, I washed the blood from his wounds and I called George to ask him to help me to put —to help me with my brother.

And he came, a man of softness and of strength and we drove him to Bridgeport to the asylum. All the way there he was handcuffed to one of us and I can still feel his eyes aimed at the back of my neck when I drove—and no one talked, yet I heard so much. The last ten miles was on a forgotten brick road and on it the tires screamed. And when we got there and he was settled and admitted, I threw my arms around him and I told him I'd be back soon to get him out and he stood still—not even my embrace had touched him.

Then they took him away. He walked on the grass to the red brick building where 200 eyes watched me through barred windows and I heard a scream and I was not sure if it was from the ward or from myself.

And every day for twenty years I saw him walk slowly like a clock from the car to that red-barred wall of eyes and not once did he turn around or wave or say I understand, you want to help me. And every time I saw that scene something inside of me stiffened and the inside of my mouth tasted like fur. This I knew every day until he went AWOL and put a bullet through his head.

When I first found out, I didn't know whether to laugh or cry. I wanted to do both, I wanted some kind of emotion to come but none would and I stood there, a piece of plastic, like he did when he was admitted and I knew we were more brothers than I wanted to believe. I saw all my promises turn to lies—now immutable. I remember all my plans for his rehabilitation and how they never were quite really more than plans—and I would tell them to him in my letters, not for him, but for myself and always I would let something come between them and reality, and I saw how my visits became fewer and fewer until the presents I sent to him for his birthday and Christmas no longer fit him and he would trade them with other patients.

At the funeral I saw George again and we bored each other with news of our families. And we shook many forgotten hometown hands and we were all surprised that the casket was open and we remarked how good he looked and how nice his color was and nobody said how they didn't know he had gotten so fat.

The preacher spoke and I sat next to the widow and was one of the pall bearers and we laid him away, one of God's children, and we remarked when we were leaving how long it had been since we had seen one another and we made forgotten plans for us to visit and I left stiffly, remembering how funerals were to comfort the living who had mistreated the deceased.

I stepped back into my eight to five day and I left my grief hung on a wilting blossom at the foot of his grave and I eased myself back into the routine in which my brother would rather have died than lived. And I remembered one night when I was eleven and he was nine and we were walking home from the ball game in the dark and we had played together on the same team and won, and on that clear night he told me he wanted to jump up, and to jump up, and to jump up high into the sky, and if he couldn't be a star, he didn't want to be nothing at all.

(April 16, 1968)

JULIE'S LAST WORD

In my sketchy account of this class I have not shown how much fun we had. The humor of these sensitive, perceptive, ordinary people was almost always pointed and topical, and the wit never went unappreciated at that table. Maybe Julie Teitelbaum should have the last word because she seldom spoke or recognized her power to impress others. When we engaged in word play one day for practice, she wrote:

"*I don't know what the word* apathy *means, and I don't care.*"

I was forced to look newly at the whole system in which I had moved for so many years like a bearing, smoothly and mindlessly.

Examination

EXAMINATION

Semester after semester, my writing classes now go like that, whether made up of freshmen, seniors, or M.A. candidates. These supposedly dull middle-class people—how could I have found them so lifeless year after year? No mystery now. They had been writing Engfish steadily, like this:

Mr. Spencer is the type of man who shows a great interest in the lives of the boys attending Pencey Prep. Being a very old man, he has seen many boys come and go at Pencey, all of them different. Each boy creates a new challenge and Mr. Spencer enjoys coping with these challenges.

That was the way students used to write for me about a book as loosey-goosey as *The Catcher in the Rye*. Mr. Spencer was a type of man. He showed great interest in the lives of the boys. He was a very old man and so he had seen a lot of boys. They were coming and going at the school, and damned if they weren't all different. Each was a challenge and old Spencer did the right thing with challenges—he coped with them. That's what the student said in his paper.

Like most Engfish paragraphs, that one about Mr. Spencer is not only chopped cardboard in its style, but it doesn't tell any truth about the book. Old Spencer didn't really like the boys; he just pretended to. And he didn't cope with them, he slobbered around making all the wrong moves. He asked Holden if he blamed him for flunking him and offered the boy a cup of hot chocolate.

A LIBERAL EDUCATION

All my adult life I had called myself and my professor friends *liberals*. And that's what we had been in the sense the term has taken on since blacks in America began to speak up. Working in a so-called Liberal Arts program dedicated to liberalizing students, I had been a member of the liberal American Association of University Professors which protected academic freedom and the American Civil Liberties Union which protected free expression, and a member—and sometime president—of a small band of angry men in the American Federation of Teachers local at Michigan State University.

None of these activities made any difference in the performance of university students.

Now I see the central sickness of liberal education. It hopes and promises, but doesn't deliver. That doesn't mean the liberal teachers are ill-intentioned, simply blind.

EVIDENCE

In the department secretary's office one of my friends said, "I suppose you're dittoing up student writing as usual. I wish I had your faith in what students can do."

"There's the evidence," I said. "But few teachers around here are interested."

"Well," he said, "They believe your program can't reach every student in class."

I thought how my earlier courses in writing had reached none of the students and wondered if these teachers were having the same success. "The program can," I said, "if the student stays with the program and carries it through."

At that point a student office worker interrupted me. "*You can't* teach *anyone to write.*"

"Some of us are," I said, "or at least freeing every student so he writes something we all want to read."

"*But you can't* teach *writing*," she said.

"Where did you learn that?"

"*I read it in a book in my Teaching of English course.*"

FROM SUCCESS TO SUCCESS

I wished the girl who believed you can't teach writing had been in the class I have just presented. On opening day I entered the room, found fifteen persons seated around the large rectangle made of three tables, and said the usual:

"Every student in this class who stays with the program will write at least one paper that knocks out the other students. Most will write several that deserve publication on campus.

"You will write, and your papers will be read around this table. The class is designed to move you from success to success. For the first month neither you nor I will talk about anything weak in the papers. Only the strong places. I will reproduce sentences or passages I think are strong and you will say why you like a passage, or just that you like it and don't know why. If you are not moved by the writing, you will say nothing.

"Keep your papers in one folder. I will not grade them until the end of the semester. In the meantime you will be getting more responses to your work than you ever got from a grade. Good writing will be reproduced and read. And praised. Later in the semester we will comment on weaknesses as well as strengths. If at any time you feel desperate for a grade, because Dad has promised you a new car if you get a B or you need a grade for application to Harvard Law School, bring the folder and I will give it a grade as of the moment.

"In this class I'm asking for truth, not Engfish (I had explained the fish, through examples). To ask such a thing is dangerous. It implies the asker habitually tells the truth. I don't. Nobody does. But in this class I will make a hard try at it, and I want you to, also."

THE FREE PURSUIT OF TRUTH

The university is dedicated to it and organized to prevent it.

How could a student feel he's freely pursuing truth sitting in a large room listening to a man lecture every day? While he's taking a multiple-choice, machine-scored test to see whether he remembers the textbook or the lecture? While he's writing essay answers to questions he didn't think up himself?

Academic freedom

I had always known that when professors are crossed by administrators, parents, or state legislators they say, "You're infringing on academic freedom." Once in a while they defend a student's right to say or print something on campus, but ordinarily it is their own freedom they consider academic and deserving of protection.

Professors seldom, if ever, think of academic freedom for students in their own classrooms. There they are in charge, not the university president or dean. They ask the questions and give the assignments. They will exercise the freedom.

Intercourse in the classroom

All through my career I had wondered why some of my colleagues—thoughtful, balanced men—required their students to buy and discuss in the classroom books like Henry Miller's *Tropic of Capricorn* and Nabokov's *Lolita*. I knew the good people in the community were seldom upset by the farts and pricks and vile standing tucks in Chaucer and Shakespeare (they didn't read the pages, just paid passing homage to them) but Miller and Nabokov wrote in contemporary language and wore no laurel wreaths. The professors risked a great deal for these writers.

I believe that English professors must fight censorship and protect the right of artists to speak freely. But now I see they choose shocking contemporary works partly to try to stir their students out of their apathy. The professor assigns a book he thinks will wake up his students without realizing their glazed eyes are the result of the drugs he has administered in the classroom—term papers with required outlines and footnotes, pop quizzes, true-false questions, and always—lectures. The student has small chance of enjoying intellectual intercourse in the classroom, so he is given physical intercourse in the books.

Closed-circuit instruction

And then in this age of television, what do they put on TV?—lectures.

One lecture after another after another

In the courtyard outside a window in Sangren Hall the snow covers everything, even the stark iron art figure in the far corner. It looks so quiet and so soft out there. "England at that point found herself in a rather uncomfortable position because her timber resources were being depleted." The snow just keeps falling and swirling in the wind, building up a new white layer, and I just want to run out into it, lie on my back, and make snow angels, moving my arms up and down and my legs in and out. "John Ralph developed a rather modern tobacco from the Caribbean leaf and introduced it into Virginia." The evergreen is leaning over from the weight of the snow and I wonder if this year we shall be blizzarded upon again and have a few days off. Probably no one even thought to dig out that evergreen with all the digging out they did last winter. "The mother country must supply the colonies with the goods they need which they cannot manufacture themselves." It looks so warm outside with all that white snow falling and making the world into a bowl of cotton candy. If I went out there and spun some around a paper funnel I wonder if he would stop lecturing long enough just to try one bite.

Joan Booth

Fellow seekers

From *University Policies and the Faculty*, 1968, p. 26:

> . . . (A superior teacher) establishes a degree of empathy with his students on two levels: first, as a *fellow seeker of truth and knowledge;* and secondly, as an interested fellow man.

Time honored

The university catalog states:

The study of English has a time-honored place in the university as a force to increase a student's sensitivity to art, to people, and to language.

A force

Engfish professors call students who write "He don't" or "We was" illiterate. Frequently black students write that dialect of American-English. The professors call it *an error.*

Few black students major in English or take courses in literature or writing. They're not prepared for them. They don't know Engfish.

Sensitivity to language

For decades white Americans have livened their language by introducing into it expressions from the streets and nightspots of Harlem, part of the dialect of supposedly ill-educated black Americans.

Sensitivity to people

I remember now that when Martin Luther King, Jr., was assassinated, the white, college-educated mayor of Memphis spoke hypocrisies in Engfish and the black garbage workers spoke truths eloquently.

Models

The professor who wants his student to increase his "sensitivity to art, to people, and to language," calls his textbook *A Program for Effective Writing.*

There is no word the student has heard more and been impressed with less than *effective,* unless it be *important.*

THE ART OF PERSUASION

Bad writing occurs in textbooks on writing by the most sophisticated and intelligent professors. The reason is simple, and dark, and frightening, like the reason for many murders—the author does not remember his readers are persons, with powers.

From Chapter 1 of *A Rhetoric Case Book,* a widely used text:

> You of course already know a good deal about rhetoric. In your earlier English courses you learned that clarity, interest, and vigor are marks of good writing. In learning the uses of the dictionary you discovered how to achieve greater clarity, interest, and vigor in the use of words.

All lies. Meant to be polite, not insulting; but the deepest kind of hypocrisy—to say that English teachers taught the student what in fact they prevented him from achieving in the classroom—clarity, interest, and vigor in writing.

THE PURPOSE OF ENGFISH

The grade school student is told by his teacher that he must learn Engfish because the high school teacher will expect mastery of it. The high school student is told by his teacher that he must learn it because the college professor will expect mastery of it. The college undergraduate is told by his professor that he must learn it so he can go to graduate school and write his Ph.D. thesis in it.

Almost no one reads Ph.D. theses.

You know what you have to know,
but still you don't know.

TESTIMONY

THE SCENE

No novel or autobiography has told fully how the university student feels as he sits in the classroom—another proof the experience benumbs and threatens. Is that because the whole educational system from university to kindergarten implies that this dullness will be the tone of the student's experience beyond graduation, and the society would never allow one of its members to demonstrate such a truth? The conspiracy of silence among students is like the conspiracy of silence among blacks. That one lasted three hundred years.

One of the first slaves in my classes to break that silence when given a chance to write freely was Mike Robb, a young veteran of Navy service. In the second week of the semester he wrote:

One of my roommates quit school today, the second week of the new semester. He only needed about twenty more hours to graduate with a four-year degree. Couldn't stand the pressure. He had worked a long time towards the degree—about five years. He wasn't dumb, but slow in understanding. He studied six hours a day. He finally met his match, though. An instructor in Industrial Technology—Dynamics. It wasn't a personality clash—just a few minor problems—completely unintelligible writing on the chalkboard, and constant mumbling, which if understood couldn't be related to the text, or the course, for that matter. I can picture him from my roommate's two-hour description. He would be smug in his own image of the learned scientist who must relate some of his vast store of knowledge to these peasants sitting before him. He has to grade on a curve, 23-20, A; 20-16, B; etc. His goal seems to be complete discouragement of ambition. Ask a question and get the "My God! Are you really that dumb?" type of answer. That is, he will explain a basic in exaggerated simplification and make you feel the Compleat Ass. In a class like that you learn by the third week not to ask questions.

I urged Mr. Robb to keep a journal during his four years and produce a biography of a college student.

Western Civilization

Another freshman turned in this free writing:

I've read The Plague *(a novel by Albert Camus), selections from* Readings in Western Civilization, *and various other artful and academic masterpieces. I learned nothing. Oh, I absorbed facts, of course, but a sponge dries out eventually. There are thirteen hours of credit marked down by my name somewhere in an overloaded file. It's a fact, but it means nothing. Thirteen hours, thirteen words, thirteen particles of dust, blown and not remembered. My teacher patrols the front of his room and spurts out random syllables. I duck, and he misses, like a rotten apple thrown at a queen—disgusting. I'd rather break windows. Windows are real. I see the flag raised and hear the anthem—nice, very nice.* [The last phrase echoes the title of a satirical film about the state of the world, produced by the National Film Board of Canada.] *Things can be so true and so nice. It makes me laugh, ha, ha.*

If a few years ago I had read a student complaining he had learned nothing from a novel by Albert Camus (even one I found slow and heavy-handed), I would have thought him stupid. Now I understand he reads any book in a university class within the total context of a system that has blasted him with minutiae and dried him out with boredom. A book by Camus is not a novel, but an assignment. Another experience like waiting in line to register, listening to roll call, filling in the space in the test booklet. The boy who said he learned nothing from reading *The Plague* is intelligent. I know him. Angry. Tomorrow he will probably be apathetic.

When I showed comments like these to other students, they began to contribute their own. I had thought they might center upon the dullness of the English classroom, but they found tedium throughout the university.

ECONOMICS 182

I walked into the Economics room on the third day of class and wormed my way to one of the seat-desk cages. I had to hitch in sideways and slide down at an angle that left my dignity and my skirt up in the air. The fellow sitting next to me was rolling a pencil between his hands. He must have been fascinated by the process because it was the only place he looked. Whenever someone came through the door, the girl in front of me looked up, then down again quickly to the book on her lap.

The graying man, who had been listed in the course catalog as 'Staff,' entered the room with his stooped shoulders and heavy briefcase. Taking out a sheaf of papers, he said, "I'll just call roll again."

I looked out the window at the window across the court.

"Allen."

"Here."

I wondered why they built the building three stories high around the square...

"Brainard."

"Here."

... stoned the ground. .

"Crandall."

"Here."

... grew the trees...

"Jones."

"Here."

... and locked the doors.

"Krane."

"Here."

They must lock the doors...

"Lawrence."

"Here."

... there was never anyone on the benches.

"O'Connor."

"Here." Here, here, every day here.

One girl used to say 'Present.' Today she said 'Here.'

"I'll just take a minute for those who've added this course, to repeat..."

I could see one person through that other window.

"And again ... the Wall Street Journal *..."*

If I concentrated, I could see three deep into the window across the court.

I looked at the clock. Fifteen minutes had gone by.

"Now I'd like to tell you how I deal with absenteeism. After three absences, your grade is dropped." He smiled and looked around the room. "When you are employed and you take time off the job, your employer loses money and efficiency. It's a matter of economics. Oh, but you say, 'I'm mature, I'm in college, I can choose for myself whether to come to class or not.' But when you choose not to come to class, you show that you're not mature at all. Staying away from class is not a sign of maturity."

The door quietly opened and closed. Coming in late for class is like coming late for church. You have to sit up in the front row.

He began again. "So—economically speaking. . ."

I wished he would.

". . . three absences. . ."

I wondered if the book that girl was reading was an Econ book. I looked at the clock. Thirty-five minutes gone.

"Are there any questions?"

A voice from the last row said, "But what if you're really sick for more than three days?"

"Well, special circumstances will call for special handling. For instance. . ."

The course catalog should have read 'Staffed.'

TEACHING AND LEARNING (EDUCATION 300)

At the first meeting of this class that met one night a week for three hours, Teacher gave us a complete schedule that we should stick to for the following fifteen weeks, then he started to lecture. About an hour later, he gave us a five-minute break. This was a disappointment to me because that meant we would have to go two hours straight without any relief for things that get tired of sitting.

After a very quick cigarette, I seated myself and prepared for the two hours ahead. An hour and a half later, Teacher was still feeding information to us as fast as we could write. I felt so pushed I wanted to jump up and run around the room screaming obscenities. My classmates were shifting around in their seats and looked as if they were drinking concentrated lemon juice. Finally it got so ridiculous that everyone started snickering. We had been pushed beyond a certain point and everyone saw the complete stupidity of the situation. Teacher tried to console us by saying, "I realize that I am trying to give you a lot of information, but we must stick to our schedule."

Organic Chemistry

When I returned to school for the fall semester, I really looked forward to my first Organic. And there I sat among over a hundred not so eager students waiting for our noble instructor to arrive. The students talked. I listened.

"He only passed a fourth of the class last year."

"He is a great teacher, but you have to already have a B.S. in chemistry to pull an A in here."

Criticisms were coming from every direction. I was drowning in an ocean of pessimistic students. Our instructor arrived, handed out lecture schedules, test dates for the semester, called the roll, and proceeded to validate the charges the students had shouted before he entered. I was actually sick after that fifty minutes of eyebrow raising, groans, and the gasping of a hundred students. I glanced at my assignment sheet and discovered that we were going to be given three chances to exhibit what we would learn from this course.

"To make a contented slave,
you must make a thoughtless one. . .
He must be able to detect
no inconsistencies in slavery.
The man who takes his earnings must
be able to convince
him that he has a perfect right to do so."

Frederick Douglass, *Life ana Times*

SLAVERY

Slaves

A couple of years ago I read the complete *Life and Times of Frederick Douglass*, a man I had long admired. He told of being sent to a professional slave-breaker known for his ability to crush the spirit of young men grown too thoughtful and independent. Looking back on receiving the full treatment, Douglass said:

> My natural elasticity was crushed, my intellect languished; the disposition to read departed, the cheerful spark that lingered about my eye died out. . .

An apt description of students sitting row after row before the lecturer in American universities. Walk down the hall and look in the open doors.

They must be kept captive

A student told me one of his professors customarily took roll both before and after the ten-minute break in the middle of a two-hour class.

And know they are inferior

I walked down a hall and saw a professor lecturing to a class of three students. He was standing at the lectern, reading from a book or his notes. The students sat in the front row before him, looking up.

LAZY AND SLEEPY IN THE FIELD

I was watching the second hand sweep around the clock while the minute hand crawled forward. The warm sun, the sweeping second hand, and the teacher's calm voice lulled me. It was 3:25 when my unconscious registered a change of tone in that voice and realized it was beginning the day's lecture.

"Now where did we leave off? I think we were just discussing Marlowe's development of. . ."

I listened spasmodically to the familiar considerations of conflict, development, cause, effect, resolution. Occasionally the class was asked to contribute, but their response was dull. They were accustomed to the fact that any original thinking on their part would be answered by, "Of course, that's possible. One person's opinion is as good as another's and I'm not saying I'm always right, but. . ."

I began to figure out how many more English classes I would have to take to finish a major. I added the column of figures on the margin of my notebook among the other doodles. "Only twelve more hours and I'll be through. Three classes."

Now the fraternity man in front of me was passing secret notes to the sorority woman on his right. The boy at my side was concentrating on writing a letter in his notebook without being seen. When I wasn't listening to the lecture, I watched the graceful flow of his handwriting or stared out the window at nothing and thought about the paper I had just gotten back.

The boy signed his letter with a flourish, turned a few pages over, and began to take cryptic notes on what was being said. I thought of the letter I had just gotten from my mother. "Why don't you tell me more about classes? How are you doing?"

THEY STEAL

Slaves and other "inferior" people not only lie, but steal. The professor of Engfish knows how to set up the course so the assignment is to borrow, and under such disheartening pressures that stealing seems the only quick and sensible out. The required research paper, with all its trivial impedimenta, is senseless, and so the student steals for the same reason the soldier steals in the army—to cheat the system that is robbing him of his humanity.

Two years ago a freshman in my class wrote a story of how he used to hand wrestle with his father. At first he lost all the time; eventually the day came when he was victor. The defeat hurt both his father and him. My student was a football player who had broken away from Engfish before many other students in the class. His first papers showed remarkable sensitivity. I posted the story on the bulletin board near my classroom. That night a colleague called to ask whether that was one of my students' papers.

"Yes," I said.

"It's plagiarized," he said. "No doubt. We've got him."

"I can't believe it."

"I've got the story right here," he said, "in a junior-high textbook." He sounded both jubilant and vindictive. I felt sick partly because I remembered sensing those feelings in myself in past years. That boy was too good a writer to have stolen anything. I knew from his other papers that he had found his own authentic voice. I asked to see the story and when I compared the two, found them close in pattern. In one the contest was wrestling on the floor; in the other, arm wrestling. The two passages which were closest went like this:

> So for nearly a year they had not wrestled, but he thought about it one night at dinner. He looked at his father closely. It was queer, but his father didn't look nearly as tall or broad-shouldered as he used to. He could even look his father straight in the eyes now.

Not a powerful paragraph. Weak, unconsidered repetitions of the words *look* and *father,* no sharpness or distinction anywhere. The other version:

> *I really grew the next four years. When I was fifteen, my father had grown small enough so that I was looking him in the eyes.*

A concise passage, with a pointed surprise in the phrasing of the last sentence. The second passage was my student's and his whole story was firmer than the professional's—no sentimentality, but a good charge of feeling. I asked the boy if he knew of the other story. He said no, and would not go along with any suggestion he might have read it long ago and been influenced. By then I didn't care whether he had been or not. If he used it as a source, as Shakespeare wrote almost every one of his plays, I could only praise his skill in improving upon the original. Five years ago I would have devoted many hours to exposing him as an impostor.

JAIL DOORS

For the new classroom building, we professors planned a lounge where students could sit in comfortable chairs, listen to tapes of plays and poetry readings, read magazines and books, and smoke. We called it The Center for English Studies so the legislators would feel it was academic and moral.

For months after it was opened, almost no students used it. A look in the main door revealed only a counter flanked with audio visual equipment and a long bookcase filled with dull covered books. Apparently students presumed it was a supply room or a teachers' lounge.

I asked one of my classes to tour the room and tell me why no students used it. "*Never knew it existed,*" one boy said. A girl pointed out that the two doors to the room, unlike others in the building, were made of steel, each with a small window reinforced with fine wire. "*Jail doors,*" she said. "*We get the message. Students are expected to steal things from this room.*"

Another girl walked around and said the white empty walls should be filled with bright paintings. Another student said the books looked dead and there were no magazines. They all liked the furniture and soft carpeting.

I was appointed to the faculty committee to do something about the Center. I came on mad, saying the place was a disgrace, intended for students, but they either didn't know it was there or were repelled when they walked in.

I suggested students should decide what to put in the room—which magazines and books and paintings. My remark horrified my colleagues. They began discussing how to prevent the thirteen volume *Oxford English Dictionary* from being stolen. Where could we put it in the room where the students couldn't get at it easily?

"And the tape recorders and phonographs," said one professor. "You know many of them have disappeared from our department in the last few years."

"Yes," I said, "faculty took them. And anyway, all the valuable machines are now kept behind the counter where an attendant checks them in and out. The room was designed that way." I became so angry I shut up.

Later that day stepping in the office tower elevator, I met one of the professors who had been upset by my suggestions. He told me of a cartoon whose punch line read "Student Lover!"

"It reminded me of you," he said.

I walked to class thinking back twenty years.

Freedom Ride

Twenty years before this date, I was studying for an M.A degree in North Carolina, when Bayard Rustin and several other CORE workers were arrested for participating in the first Freedom Ride testing segregation on buses. I attended the trial and decided to take my own ride home for vacation.

I got on a bus in Chapel Hill, took a place next to a black woman on the long rear seat, and was told by the driver the law forbid me to sit there. I insisted I was traveling interstate, and federal law applied. Far out in the country, he stopped the bus near a power substation and left us to make a phone call. When he returned to the bus, he started up and drove off. I kept expecting him to stop for a rendezvous with a couple of men in a car pulled up alongside the highway. We reached Charlottesville, Virginia, without incident. When I stepped down from the bus, three big drivers were standing at the door. I tensed myself ready to ward off blows. Not one of the three moved. As I walked by, the biggest said in a whisper, "Nigger Lover."

YASSUH, COLONEL

Slaves know how to act. At the beginning of the semester the sharpest, most knowing tarry after class and say to the master,

"*Is it* Doctor? *or* Professor?"

They know the ego of teachers. In his *Autobiography* Malcolm X tells how the shoe shine man or lavoratory attendant in the hotel makes a few light but firm passes of the whiskbroom across the back of the man he has served, not to remove lint, but to remind him he has been paid deference by a servant.

I'M JUST A SIMPLE DARKY

In most classes you take you usually have some idea of the grade you're going to receive by the tests you've taken. But what happens when you don't have any tests? You worry, that's what you do. You try not to miss class because he might take that into consideration when he gives you a grade, but most of all you try to get to know your teacher better. Become friends, talk about dogs and cats and other things that interest teachers. Nod your head when he speaks in class, show him you're listening, and you think he's right on the point he's making. But don't overdo it. He may be wise enough to spot the brown-noser, the kid who constantly visits his office and talks about home, animals, and good books.

Another thing you can do is compliment him on his dress. "Sharp suit you've got on today, Mr. So and So." They like that. It makes them think their Robert Hall outfit looks like a Petrocelli original. (Give yourself one point.)

Try to run into your teacher outside the classroom, especially at shopping centers and cultural events. It makes you look good and teachers usually like it when they're addressed formally in front of other people. (Score two points.)

Be simple in language. If you use a word he doesn't know, subtract one point and hit yourself in the head. Teachers like to think they know it all, so don't stump them on a word. Also, make sure your personal hygiene is adequate, meaning if you have bad breath, use a mouth wash before talking to him, shower every few days, and if your feet stink, use powder.

So after all of this preparation, you finally go up to your teacher and say, "Mr. So and So, could you give me some indication of my final grade?"

If the reply is "Well, you've got nothing to worry about," ask for a specific indication—A,B,C,D, or F. Be firm but don't be pushy.

If he still evades you, say "Coprophagous," and walk out.

Assuming your teacher is a little upset, he'll probably finger through his dictionary and find out what "coprophagous" means. If you're wondering what it means, the simple definition is "Eat shit."

THEY NEED CORRECTION

English professors customarily bridle at a social gathering when they hear the remark, "Oh, an English teacher! I'll have to watch my grammar!"

The professors are insulted. They would never correct anyone's grammar in public.

They forget the classroom is public.

THEY ARE IGNORANT

I was conversing with a colleague, an old friend, when into the office stormed one of the most distinguished and published members of the department. He slammed down his books and said with a sigh, "Oh, my God! These kids don't know a thing. They haven't read anything. I really can't talk to them."

My friend said, "George, don't forget you were a student once yourself."

There was no answer. I didn't see how there could be.

ILLITERATE

She has that look that Mrs. Erikson had in the fourth grade. The look of the eagle. My drill instructor in the Marines had it; he could spot someone out of step from a block away and he'd just zero in with those eyes and you were in step.

Mrs. Erikson used to go around the fourth grade whacking us with the ruler to supplement the look. This lady can't do that, so the look improves. Just sitting in the back of the class there dreaming of the open road and zap!—the dreaded stare has struck. I can't stand it and look down at my notebook.

Mrs. Erikson said, "You be here or else," and we were there. This lady stands with hands clasped in front of a non-bosom and says we should be here every day or we will miss something important . . . only major catastrophes should keep you from class. . . Giggle, Ha Ha. Funny.

Who are you trying to shit, Grandma? We don't fall for your disguised orders. I'll come when I damn well feel like it.

"Now are there any questions?"

Yes. May I stand up here in the back of the room from where I receive your hawkish, deadly stares and scream and go running out the door, down the stairs, out the door, across the parking lot, and up that grassy little hill to relieve a little of the pressure that has been building up over the years?

Up in her office after flunking a test, I sit down and clear my throat and she says, "Tom, what are we going to do with you?"

We ain't going to do nothing with me, Baby. She starts to explain all the groovy things I do not know, that she loves, and my mind and eye go out the slit of a window from which she fires arrows on illiterates below. I come inside again and look at her and wonder when the games will end.

She looks up from a gerund and gives me a stare at close range. You pay attention or I will kick you in the shin with my open-toed Minnie Mouse shoe, or maybe I will just stare at you.

Please not that, God. A little voice within me says that the games will never end . . . never. And the little voice reels back in his chair and laughs uncontrollably with his hands clasped over his fat belly.

Naive

Today I remembered a meeting of several years ago—it was called for English majors. We professors asked them to write down any suggestions they had for our courses. One said, "*Why not read some contemporary poetry we like? I suggest Allen Ginsberg.*"

Those of us looking over the response smiled condescendingly when one professor read that comment to us, and I thought how little I would like to spend several weeks on Allen Ginsberg with a class. I had to allow the man wrote some lively lines in *Howl*, but overall he bored me with his self-conscious attempts to shock. Just like a slave to make a suggestion so wrongheaded.

Later when I was re-reading Walt Whitman, I thought how much I liked him and how bad he was at times. And then I knew I had looked at the student's suggestion perversely. He could bring *Howl* to class and I could bring Walt's babaric yawp and we could compare them. No reason to demand either of us give up our favorite, but we might in our conversations learn to see more (or less) in our poet's work because we had read the other.

Most students are not my equal in experience or knowledge of literature and writing. But in some aspects of each they may be my superior. I will never know until I let them bring forth themselves full of their own experiences and ideas and feelings, as they are forced to let me bring forth myself.

Should I grade the student in that class in Ginsberg and Whitman? The only defensible move would be to grade each other, and that seems a waste of time, a daily curse upon our meetings.

LET THEM KNOW WHERE THEY STAND

After my class on the first day of the semester, I found lying on one of the seats a dittoed memorandum to students, part of which said:

> ASSIGNMENTS: For each assigned book you must turn in a statement of thesis for each chapter or section of each book. All thesis statements should begin, "The thesis of chapter—is. . . . ."
>
> ATTENDANCE: I expect you to be in attendance at all class meetings. It is my choice as to how to handle absences. Since absence can affect the grade a person receives, I am sure you will want to take this into consideration before being absent.
>
> PARTICIPATION: As I expect you to be in class, I also expect you to participate in class discussions. My teaching method is to get at important aspects of the subject matter through discussion. The dialogue is really the heart of the class. I expect you to contribute; if you don't there are penalties involved. If you are the intelligent, but "strong and silent type," I suggest that you find a class or an instructor that better suits your silence and recalcitrance . . .
>
> PHILOSOPHY: The best teaching and learning goes on between a teacher interested in his students and his subject, and students who are interested in learning what the teacher has to profess (hence, professor). Through dialogue, two minds ought to be able to seek clarity and truth. Both student and teacher are here in the academic community for the same purpose—to gain and test knowledge, that is our purpose this semester.

Remember they can't think for themselves

You will consult at least fifteen separate sources, half of which are books, and half periodicals. Take notes on 4 x 6 cards, not 3 x 5, and be prepared to present them upon demand. Bibliography and footnotes will follow the MLA Style Sheet. At least one thousand words, with a cover sheet that includes a statement of purpose. The paper should have a clearly indicated introduction, body, and conclusion. Do not use the word "I" except in the conclusion of the paper.

Those instructions should be sufficient to tell the student the professor is interested only in the form of what he says.

Climbing the wall

There is a yellow page of a newspaper trying to get out of a corner and away from the wall of our dorm. The wind won't let it. It bends and does contortions like a body mechanics class and then it just stretches out face down in the snow. It tries to climb the walls and up the rough bricks, but only gets a little way before the wind hauls it down again. It tries to sneak into the light, but something whips it closer to the wall and folds it against its will. It has been flapping around in that corner all day long like a student trying to avoid going to the library to do research.

Margaret Stevens

Use the whip

The Engfish professor uses spelling as a whip. He doesn't mean to. Says it's a minor consideration—of *mechanics*. No matter that he knows English spelling wasn't standardized until Samuel Johnson's dictionary in 1755, and that before then Shakespeare and the poet Richard Lovelace and John Donne, Dean of St. Paul's Cathedral, and all their learned contemporaries spelled freely, writing *doe* for *do* or *hee* for *he* according to their whims. No matter. The professor still marks unstandardized spelling with red ink and lowers the student's grade with a vengeance or sanctimonious pity. In the seventeenth century, Lovelace wrote:

> I cannot tell who loves the Skeleton
> of a poor Marmoset, nought but boan, boan.
> Give me a nakednesse with her cloath's on.

And everyone knew what he was saying then, and everyone knows now. But English spelling became fixed and almost impossible to learn, and Engfish teachers learned it and set themselves apart. They are not today going to give up that advantage over the unwashed, the careless, and the lazy.

Today professors resist the introduction into the schools of ITA (The Initial Training Alphabet), a beautiful 44-character phonetic spelling alphabet with which six-year-olds write exciting notes to each other and the teacher instead of sentences like "My name is Tom. I have a Daddy and a Mommy." The professors would never consider letting everything hang out, as Goldie says, and go back to spelling carelessly, but effectively, as Shakespeare did.

Sin

A person who has never been an English teacher cannot realize how hard it is for an expert to see spelling and punctuation as secondary matters. There is the sentence: *I had too horse's*" and never mind how brilliantly a student has brought the horse's alive in his paper, the errors must be called to his attention. Matter of morality. Sin. Correction is a holy duty Can't pass by the words without circling them in blood. No sir. Can't take them lightly and say, "Isn't it interesting that you use an apostrophe for a plural ending in s, just like Lovelace (cloath's) and other writers of the sixteenth and seventeenth centuries?"

The student gets the idea. "*All those corrections show he's more interested in my spelling than in what I say. So I won't bother to say anything I really mean.*"

PUBLICIZE THEIR ERRORS

Engfish teachers pass around to each other what they call "bloopers" made by students in their papers. They post them on bulletin boards. They send them to teachers' magazines, which publish them as humorous material to fill empty spaces in their pages. Three of the commonest slips printed are:

1. *His parents were having martial trouble.*
2. *He took it for granite.*
3. *The boys were studing in the lounge of the girls' dormitory.*

In the column heading of a recent issue of an English teachers state association newsletter appeared the word CALENDER. In the graduate school I attended the English Department distributed to faculty and students a notice containing the word GRAMMER. These bloopers were not posted or printed in magazines as filler.

TEACH THEM USEFUL THINGS

The English Department in any university performs a service for the whole institution. It replaces the student's own language with Engfish and thus equips each young scholar for writing papers in any field of study. Appropriately, Freshman Composition is frequently referred to by professors as a "service course."

ERASABLE

Today I realized why university bookstores sell students a special paper whose chief virtue is hiding erasures. The paper is priced high (four times as much as that used for the manuscript of this book), so the student will understand the first essential in school writing—to avoid spelling and punctuation errors. The typing paper is perfect for Engfish purposes. Ink does not take well on it. It can be erased easily. It is a poor medium for communication.

DON'T LET THEM GET UPPITY

Found in the hall near a classroom used for the Humanities course:

Letters to students:
(Nr. 8)

I would like to make one thing absolutely clear:

Shoddy essays mirroring shoddy thought will not obtain a passing degree.

Shoddy thought indicated that the student concerned did not cooperate to reach a reasonable degree of EFFICIENCY LEVEL; and that his INFORMATION LEVEL is completely unsatisfactory.

> Dean and Area Chairman rightly insist on essays being properly planned, well arranged and written in fluent good English that a university student of medium ability should master without difficulty.
>
> Essays should not be written in a way that avoids all study and effort and, superficially, gives the impression of personal conclusions as arrived "after careful consideration of underlying facts."
>
> Essays have to account for facts. Essays have to state generally accepted ideas about facts. Essays can state personal opinions or personal conclusions which do not conform with generally held views as long as some logically ordered reasoning has been added that warrants deviation in opinion or judgment of the writer of the essay concerned.

If you beg to differ in your conclusions (NOT IN THE FACTS!) state the reasons. Nobody will be penalized for having differed; on the contrary, an attempt at personal view, opinion or judgment will be considered a major asset of the essay.

Next were typed a dozen excerpts from a student paper, under the heading *Example of an essay that should never have been written*. After the excerpts, the professor, who signed his name with the title "Dr.," said, "Obviously, the essay was written to look clever and to save the bother of studying, and of preparing it properly."

Like most self-righteous communications, this one does not live up to its own standards. Its assertion "I would like to make *one* thing absolutely clear" is followed by a *number* of things. The phrase "a reasonable degree of EFFICIENCY LEVEL" is not "good English"; levels do not come in degrees.

Many slips of this kind in reproduced instructions to students are excused by professors as the work of ignorant secretaries. These professors take no responsibility for proofreading, an act they expect their students to carry out faithfully.

But the mechanical errors in this document do not offend me. I can make sense of everything. And I would excuse the professor and his secretary their slips if the professor was not so insufferably superior. I would allow my students the same errors the professor has made.

THE WHOLE FORCE OF THE DIFFICULTY

On a bench in the hall of a classroom building I found a dittoed sheet—prepared, I would guess, by an English professor for his Freshman Composition class:

Theme Topics

1. What science cannot discover, mankind cannot know.
2. Being good is wearing nose rings when nose rings are worn.
3. The widespread practice of nudism will lead to greater harmony among human beings.
4. Man created god in his own image.
5. Women who have borne more than two illegitimate children and who must seek financial aid from a tax supported agency should be sterilized.
6. War, disease and famine are necessary for the preservation of mankind.
7. Capital punishment is not an effective means of deterring crime.
8. Fraternities and sororities are democratic societies on a smaller scale.
9. Negroes are no worse than other minority groups.
10. Legalized prostitution is a necessity in our modern world.

I am sure the professor who made up that list thought he was encouraging free speculation as well as logical rigor, but the form of his topics binds the student to feelings and experience often not his own. The trickiness of such phrasing is no surprise to most students. They figure out what game they are supposed to play—what does the professor himself think about each statement he has made? I will give that back to him.

Early in my teaching career I tried to manage students in this way. And yet I worshipped John Stuart Mill, who said that a man must be able to hear opinions

> from persons who actually believe them; who defend them in earnest, and do their very utmost for them. He must know them in their most plausible and persuasive form; he must feel the whole force of the difficulty which the true view of the subject has to encounter and dispose of. . . .
>
> (*On Liberty*, 1859)

THE LOWER CLASSES

Visiting another university, I had lunch with a poet who was also a professor of creative writing. He spoke highly of the work of his graduate students, a welcome surprise to me to hear a good word about the lower classes. But he added, "And the undergraduates, they were—well, you know, undergraduates."

In his *Life and Times,* the former slave Frederick Douglass said:

> Man derives a sense of his consequences in the world not merely subjectively but objectively. If from the cradle through life the outside world brands a class as unfit for this or that work, the character of the class will come to resemble and conform to the character described. To find valuable qualities in our fellows, such qualities must be presumed and expected.

The class discussed
what to do about an incompetent
professor. I had no answer
to show how the system
had arranged to correct itself.

Overseers

Victims of the System

Today for about the tenth time in the last two years, I was scared by the thought of having this book published. What will my colleagues think? I am using what they said and did to reveal the slave system. No matter that I have shown myself one of the blindest of the overseers. They are sure to resent my exposure of them and to conclude that I think them totally evil.

At moments I look at all professors, including myself, with understanding. We are no less victims of the system than our students. In the schools we were brought up as slaves. Someone or something opened to us the possibility of becoming overseers. We submitted to the required trials, said, "Yes sir," to the professors in graduate school and moved out of slavehood. But we did not escape the system. That was not presented as a possibility. So we stayed with slavery, as overseers. Some of us acted more decently and liberally toward the slaves than others, but like the best slaveowners—Thomas Jefferson, for example—we perpetuated a system which robs young people of their selfhood.

Now I realize why the tone of this book oscillates between bitterness and charity. Writing it, I felt like the person who confronts the reality of the extermination of Jews under Hitler's regime. In Germany and elsewhere, all men who allowed that to happen, including German Jews, were responsible, but not responding. We permitted the most massive attempt at genocide ever undertaken. Where were we? What were we?

We say we didn't know. The systems, old and new, had taught us not to notice what happened to Jews. Or if we noticed, not to talk, not to stir up trouble. So there's the reasonable explanation. It must be given weight.

Yet the criminality of our neglect should be shouted to the hills.

A NICE ENOUGH PERSON

Mrs. McConnell started out the Advanced Writing class today by asking, "*What is a student's responsibility when he finds himself in a class where the professor is doing an absolutely incompetent job? Where he is a nice enough person, but simply isn't doing anything with the materials of the course? Should the student make known his inefficiency? And to whom? Would anything be done?*"

BOXES

During most of the thousand or more years of Western higher education, we professors have fulfilled our function as masters.

Once I complained to the Director of Placement of a large university where I was teaching. I said the forms for recommending students for jobs (usually as teachers) were too restrictive—Check the boxes for appearance (which came first in the list) and personality and citizenship (I was surprised to find no box for regularity of bowel movement). I received this comment in a letter from him:

> Frankly, instead of the form, I would much rather have a letter, long or short, from any one of our University staff members to place with the recommendations of graduating seniors and alumni. We attempted to secure information by this process over a period of several years. Unfortunately most faculty members failed to get any information whatever to us. Those who did, after writing about 4 or 5 recommendations, used stereotyped expressions, and within a short time, the letters became so standard that they could have been switched from one candidate's file to another.

All alike

The Placement Director's assertion that faculty recommendations made every student sound alike reminded me of an experience a friend of mine had teaching a class of Honors students.

He said that at the opening of the course he asked the students to read a book or play and write a critical, personal response to it. He looked at the papers, became disgusted, and went back to class and said, "After reading about half of your papers I saw they were all the same. I could have switched the names of the authors and no one would have known. I told you to write your honest opinion and reaction to what you read. You are all different persons, with different attitudes and experience. If you're writing half honestly, your paper will differ from every other in the class. Now quit trying to write like a standard student and give us some of your own perception and intelligence."

The papers improved. This teacher was not upholding the system.

Hiring overseers

When the university hires a teacher, most professors interviewing the experienced applicant never ask how his students are doing in his classes. He would have no rational answer. Whatever his slaves are doing, it is not something he could bring himself to describe in a conversation with an intelligent man trained in the same field. Whatever they are doing, it is not worth talking about.

EVALUATING THE PLANTATION

When the young man with a new Ph. D. looks for a job, he judges the university by the number of reputable scholars on its staff, and their reputability upon their publications. He would never think of judging a university by the performance of its students. There is no way of checking that.

In fact, the students perform nothing alive and valuable enough to be examined by an outsider. A parent bold enough to ask a professor what his students are doing is told quite truly that the answer could not be meaningful to a layman. The students' performance cannot be evaluated by anyone untrained in the complex statistics involved in scientific evaluation, or acutely aware of the fine gradations of non-performance by students. Even the experts seldom agree on the interpretation of the results of such evaluation.

That is because nothing has been learned positive enough to be measured or appreciated.

WRITING FOR THE SLAVES

The system infects everyone. A professor I know who is considered by students exceptionally human and valuable and can write outside the university with a light touch wrote the following statement to be distributed to honors students. It sounds serious and impressive, but its message could be communicated in half the number of words. In the right-hand column I have presented a short version which I think omits no vital point.

THE HONORS ESSAY	THE HONORS ESSAY
The Honors Essay is to be thought of as an attempt by the student to cope effectively with a reasonably limited but challenging critical problem.	The Honors Essay is an attempt by the student to write a reasonably limited, valuable critical paper.

The particular problem that a given student will work on shall be determined by consultation between that student and his instructor. We expect that in most cases the student himself will roughly define his problem and that the instructor's chief function will be to help the student arrive at a fruitfully limited definition of the problem. However, the instructor certainly retains the right to reject a particular proposal either because he thinks that it is not workable or because he thinks that it is so far out side his own range of com petence that he could not do an effective job ot supervising work on it. On the other hand, the student has the right to expect that the instructor will suggest a variety of problems that he might work on; the student may or may not accept such suggestions but they will at least give him useful examples of the sort of thing he should consider doing. .

Usually the student will roughly define what he proposes to write about and then get help from the instructor in sharpening and limiting it.

The instructor may reject a proposal because he thinks it unworkable or so far outside his own range that he is not competent to supervise it. The student has the right to ask for suggestions for subjects from the instructor, but he need not accept any of them.

BECOMING PREPARED TO TEACH

After the student has graduated from college with some mastery of Engfish, he can take an advanced degree in it and become a teacher. Perhaps he can become the president of the state association of English teachers and write like this in the newsletter for members:

> Fall term has begun and most of us are thinking about our school year calendars. You will want to consult the calendar of English meetings over the state which is given in this issue. . . We hope that you will *plan* to attend at least one of these area meetings, which have been *planned* to *start* you off with a boost this year. Most of these conferences *start* with a general session. . .

This is Folksy Engfish, a little flabby with its weak repetitions of *plan* and *start* (italicized by me above), the kind of writing that gives you a *boost*, never anything exciting like a *goose*—and little nasty nudges like "You *will* want to consult. . ." Teacher talk

AND DEFENDING ONE'S OWN LAZINESS

Recently a professor at the University of Michigan who assumes students are intelligent and alive (both rare assumptions by professors) wrote this sentence in the foreword to an anthology of student writings:

> Robert F—and Thomas M—earned the respect and admiration of the entire group. I cannot avoid the cliché: Both gave freely of themselves.

He could have avoided the cliché and come up with a more distinctive expression. I tell my writing students I will not allow them such sloth and immorality. To make sure they know they can do better than that, I ask them to put down some clichés and then turn them around.

In my Advanced Writing class, Margaret McNally gave me a line for beginning speeches at conferences: "*It's both a pressure and a privilege to be here.*"

A GREAT SATISFACTION

During my first seventeen years of teaching, several times someone said to me in social conversation, "It must be a great satisfaction to be a teacher—to know you're helping young people, and to have some of them come back to see you in later years."

At those moments I would sit back, startled a little by the idea, and think, "Yes, yes it really is, isn't it? I'm engaged in this noble enterprise and most other persons in the world are out grubbing for money at their dirty, selfish jobs."

Occasionally a student would write me after leaving school and say what a good teacher I had been. Invariably he would mention my sense of humor and the stories I brought into the classroom from my own experience. Sometimes he would comment on my neckties, which he considered distinctive.

At those moments I would also sit back, breathe the smug air deeply, and think that those few appreciative students were worth all the others who slipped unnoticed through my classes.

An incredibly barren experience—about 4,000 students in those years spending time with a man dedicated to improving their minds, and only a score had let him know they had enjoyed it; and even then, mainly because they and he had been attracted to each other as persons. Matter of personality.

RESPONSE TO THE THIRD WAY

Teaching the Third Way brings a different sort of comment from students. One of my former students sent me a letter reporting a conversation he had had with another member of the class.

"*I can still remember some lines from the stuff we wrote.*"

"*Remember that poem with the line about the kid sitting in the tree 'crotch to crotch'? That still kills me. It's so perfect.*"

"*And do you remember the story about the kid with his grandfather, when they killed the rabbit in the snow?*"

"*I guess we all reached some sort of a peak in that class didn't we? At least, a first peak, like the first time you make a jump-shot as a kid. Oh, you know there will be lots more, and higher, and straighter, but there will never be another first one, and you'll never be just a kid, shooting like a kid, again.*"

THE PURPOSE OF THIS COURSE

I noticed the tendency for the class to discuss the subject matter of writing more ("My grandmother was like that, too"), at times, than the actual writing. This was less true at the end of the course, but I was one of the offenders.

The comments addressed to me have helped me evaluate my own writing more objectively, reduced my incidents of redundancy and repetition (I think I just redunded), and have given my writing a better direction—I am not as concerned with my reader's desires (profs in particular) as I once was but am more conscious of my expression, honesty, and validity as a writer.

I realize that the purpose of this course is to improve the quality of student writing in other classes as well as in the creative sense. Unfortunately the scholarly work I have produced has all been turned in to other professors and not to the observant eyes of the students in the class. I should have read some of it in here and it only now occurs to me to have done it. I kick myself for this oversight.

TEACHING'S BEAUTIFUL

Teaching's beautiful—supposedly I have the "dumbest kids in the school." Some goddamn new teacher even told one class, "I checked into the school records and I see that you're the dumbest kids in the whole school." Bastard, I chewed him out.

These supposedly dumb kids certainly aren't dumb. Sure, they're crude and primitive, but on the whole they're brilliant. I found this out through their free writings.

LEARNING

The difference between the last three student comments about my teaching and those I used to receive is that they are not about me as much as about what the students wrote and how their comments improved each other's writing.

Results.

INTERSECTION

The excitement I feel from seeing students write well—whether they are my students or another teacher's—is both high and steady. I am no longer thinking, "He did so well what the book told him to do." Or, "He remembered the right answers to all the questions." I am taken into the world he has written about, and often it holds me. Sometimes I cannot detach myself from it for months, years. Then the student is no longer simply passing tests but pulling together experiences and ideas which begin to in tersect with mine.

He is more than a name on the roll for me to count. He has counted in my life.

COUNTING

Many of my New English students' comments and writings become part of the shared knowledge of my family. The other night watching CBS news I heard that a large steel corporation had been accused of favoring certain of its customers in business transactions. The company spokesman's answer was that although they had been doing nothing at all wrong, they would cease the practice immediately. I turned to my wife and said, "That reminds me of the little girl who was asked by her mother if she had thrown the waste paper in the cold air register."

Before I could give the punch line, my wife had supplied it from her memory of a student's journal entry: "*No, Mommy, I didn't see me do it.*"

The Kind You Enjoy

I said to my wife, "I'd like to read you some stuff from this magazine of student writing."

Kirk, thirteen years old, said, "From what?"

My wife said, "You know, writing done in the new program."

"Oh," said Kirk, "you mean that kind you enjoy reading."

He had identified it. The Third Way insidiously may take over the universities for that reason alone. For so long the schools and universities have produced from students such drab and dreary performance that few persons can imagine what teaching and learning can be like when life is manifested in the classroom. When it is, everyone in the enterprise begins to like himself.

Here

When Professor Henry Reifsnyder at Indiana State University sent me five copies of *Here*, a small magazine of writing from his classes and those of a colleague, Margaret Whittle, I thought I would take a quick look, but found myself reading them all. No Engfish.

Half of the stories were not memorable, but the other half had me talking to myself. One struck me because it articulated a feeling I have had: "*I think many people move away from someone who is blind as if the blindness might be contagious.*" Then the story, which told of a blind student who got no help from others in trying to find the classroom on the first day. He made his way into the room ana took a seat in the teacher's chair behind the lectern, thinking he was in the back of the room.

I liked the style of Cindy Craig's paper:

> *Right now our room looks like a pigpen. No, I guess it really doesn't look like that. A pigpen has dirt floors. We have tile somewhere down there. Besides, pigs don't drink Cokes or hang peace and love posters from their fence. Our room looks like our room.*

I had to get more copies of *Here* to show other teachers and students. Henry said I could have twenty for $4.40. I sent him the check. A year before he had sent me $5.00 for a number of copies of the magazine of student writing I put out.

Incredible. Here I was on a summer evening reading for pleasure the writing of students not my own. And two English teachers were paying their own money for such a privilege.

TEACHER POWER

To teach the Third Way is to set up an arrangement which allows the majority of students in a class to find their own powers and to increase them. Making others powerful makes the teacher feel powerful. And the power of both is a fact.

I have never before known such a feeling. There is no antagonism in it. It is not power for struggle, for besting others in intellectual or physical combat. It is akin to the feeling Gandhi had when he was chasing the British out of India and making them feel better men for it.

If the professor does his job perfectly, every student in the class should get an A.

GRADES

THROW THEM A CURVE

At Michigan State, where I taught ten years in the Department of Communication Skills, every year or so a few administrators and professors would become worried that the grade curve for the hundreds of freshman classes in speaking and writing was too steep—too many B's, not enough C's, D's, and F's. So we teachers would get together in the staff room and grade five themes. Invariably on several our grades would range from B to F. Year after year each of us wondered how the other could be such a mistaken evaluator as to give a high grade to a paper we had flunked, or vice versa.

We made an effort to count "content" in the papers more heavily than most English teachers do. But that didn't help. We still graded a single paper all the way from B to F.

Now that I understand all the papers were written in Engfish my bafflement is gone. There was no honest-to-God content in those papers. So we looked for anything hard enough to base a judgment on. Spelling. Sentence structure. One of us fixed on punctuation errors, another on topic sentences.

AN A FOR THE TEACHER

At almost every university where I have taught, including those that employed me only part-time, I have received in my faculty mail box a notice from a department head that went essentially like this:

> Everyone who taught at least one English course last fall should have received a report showing percentages of grades given on different levels and in multi-section courses as well as the percentages of the grades he gave. These figures might well make us wonder if we are not somewhat "softer" in our grading than we really should be. This is not to imply that we should establish a departmental curve requiring so many C's, D's, and E's to be given by each instructor. However, to suggest some kind of upper limit in softness, anyone who finds himself giving, with any regularity, *more* than 20% A's, less than 20% C's, and *no* D's in ordinary undergraduate classes should ask himself if his students

> are really *that* good. Anyone who fairly frequently goes beyond these limits in assigning grades may legitimately be regarded by students (and by colleagues) as a "soft touch."

Once again, the implication that the slaves come to the master as a given; they have certain abilities beyond which they cannot go; it is understood by all that the master is not going to help them improve their performance and extend their capacities.

The above message is a reasonable one to send to First Way teachers. When I taught that way for seventeen years, I was a soft touch, gave good grades that weren't deserved. Now I know that I did that out of feeling that it was indecent to treat such decent young persons—who tried to do my bidding—as failures.

But the message makes no sense at all to a person teaching the Third Way. For as he becomes more experienced in freeing them and they become more experienced in using that freedom with discipline, more and more of his students will get A for a grade.

The professor should know his students and pitch his program at a level not out of their reach or too far beneath them. Maybe a couple of students will goof off or miss class because they are sick. They can't be given A's even when the professor is doing his best. But otherwise, if he has arranged a course to teach certain knowledge and skills, and the program does not work, then his students will not get an A and low grades will prove him a poor teacher.

Overheard in the Snack Bar

I don't take advanced courses any more. Take a regular course, get an A. Works a lot better.

Failure

When I talk to colleagues about abolishing grades, most of them grow edgy. And students grow nervous thinking of the unknown. For seventeen years I was trained by the system to set up hurdles for the students and give grades on jumping. I am reminded of E. B. White's story "The Door"—"There will be no not jumping." My classes used to go like this: a test on this aspect of the poems, next week a test on another aspect, and so on through the semester until we *covered* the wide range of ways of looking at poems.

That is the First Way. Today it seems nonsense. Why set the hurdle so high the first time? So a goodly number of students will not clear it cleanly, and a few will ram into it and knock it down and bruise their shins. Only if a large number do badly will the grade distribution look right.

Jumping

Today I begin by asking students to do something they can do brilliantly right off. Then I ask them to do more difficult things. If the next hurdle is too high, I lower it, or let them try several times. This is not a test, with grades, not a chance for me to fail them and work out my aggressions or feel superior. It is a try at something, with lots of chances for failure without punishment.

The hurdles I place on the track are often hazy things, as if seen in a mist. Sometimes students see them clearly; sometimes hardly at all. Occasionally a student runs skipping or stumbling down the track in the haze and jumps twice as high as the hurdle because he wasn't sure it was there

WHAT'S YOUR HONEST FEELING?

In teaching a course in Humanities, my wife, an artist, asks students to record in journals their first impressions of an art work—a piece of music they hear, the Picasso sculpture that stands in the plaza in Chicago. Your feelings. With absolute honesty.

What is my wife to do under the present grading system when the student comes back and says what he really felt when he looked at that giant metal abstraction of a woman?

"Oh. You get a C+"?

AN INDICATION OF ONE'S ABILITY

Ford Motor Company will want to see grades before hiring a graduate. Nonsense. Ford can interview a candidate, ask him to perform acts that will give a far better idea of how valuable he will be to the firm than all the grades on his transcript, including the A he got in physics, as I did in high school, for memorizing the theorems, or whatever they were called, and passing tests on them while being unable to carry out a single laboratory experiment even with the help of the cookbook manual we were provided with. My lab partner helped me in each one.

Graduate school needs grades to determine whom to admit. Nonsense. What graduate school needs is an expectation that the students it accepts will do independent, mature work. The last place to find out whether they can do that is in a transcript of grades from undergraduate days.

Anxiety

In my university, the teachers of the Humanities course recently agreed to institute a pass-fail system which would replace conventional grading. When a history professor got wind of the insurrection, he insisted that the Faculty Senate rule on the matter. In his brief against the motion to abolish conventional grades, he said, in part:

> The rationale for the proposal explains that the staff wishes to remove "the onus threatening the student's grade point average" and reduce "the coercive function of the grade." The efforts to practically eliminate anxiety from the learning process, however well intentioned, are curiously naive. Anxiety is a necessary concomitant of life. As George Bernard Shaw put it, "Without fear we could not live a single day: if you were not afraid of being run over, you would be run over before you got home." Let us, then, determine reasonably stringent standards in our courses without attempting to remove anxiety altogether from the learning process or the subjectivity inherent in the measurement and evaluation processes of our profession.

Nothing like a little productive anxiety—perhaps anticipating a guerrilla attack in Viet Nam?

In a Third Way class a student becomes extremely anxious when he reads his paper to his peers. And whether the ensuing criticism is positive or negative, or both, the anxiety usually makes his next paper stronger. But the anxiety is not about grades from teacher. It is about how strongly his paper will affect his peers and his teacher.

And anxiety

In a Third Way writing class a student has available a response to his work almost every day. His paper may be read to the rest of the class for seminar criticism. The professor may duplicate it and bring it to class as a model of good work. He may post it on the bulletin board in the hall or publish it in several thousand copies in a magazine meant for the general student body. While the student sits in seminar thinking about and commenting on another's paper, he usually has his own paper in mind, and it is receiving his silent criticism from his own words about the other student's paper.

And so with the comments of other students around the table—what they say about his paper, they may apply to their own. The professor may comment, but the student does not have to take his opinion as law. He can judge its strength or weakness against the other comments made by the students around the table.

In the Third Way, a student gets four times as much evaluation as in a class where he receives grades.

Maturing

When I used to teach at Michigan State, I visited football practice and heard Coach Biggie Munn refer to his huge semiprofessional football players as "kids." One of the kids, a slightly balding All-American named Sam Williams, brought *his* kids to the spring college football practice. I think there were three of them.

College kids are adults and they are kids—averaging between eighteen and twenty years of age. They leave home to come to the campus, and during their sojourn there are expected to make the final break from parents.

The omission of grading in the college years would be a larger sign than any Bachelor of Arts or Science degree that students are living in that period of life when Americans come of age.

They don't want to know what you know, but what you don't know.

Questions

Tests

In the first years of my teaching my colleagues coached me on how to make up ingenious tests on which students couldn't cheat. I experienced small moments of fiendish pleasure when I created a multiple-choice question that would separate the keenest from the most mediocre minds—as I was told. But then came pass-the-tests-back day and I spent the whole hour arguing with the smartest students over why in that game their gambit had not been acceptable as the right answer. Their cleverness matched mine. And the test didn't turn out what my colleagues said it would: a useful teaching device.

Multiple-choice

The student looks at the test and says, "Damnit! *c* is right and *b* is right, but it says up above there's only one right answer."

It may be that what he has in mind is the most subtle comment of anybody in the class. Yet he can't put it down. He would like to tell why he thinks both *c* and *b* touch the question positively. In fact, neither do the whole job for him. He wants to make qualifications, to express subtle shades of meaning. That is what he is in school to learn to do. The test will not let him.

Cold

I SAW A YELLOW TEST BOOKLET
blow across the parking lot
beneath my window.
The pages were fluttering
as the book bounced
along with the snow.
The wind died for a
second; it lay there,
heaving a little.
A car drove over
the book and it was pulled
along in the vacuum.
It looked solitary and
remote out there, cold—
a yellow booklet.
From the end of
a pencil you impart
all truth and knowledge
in the scholarly Dick
and Jane style and
hand in your hour
with faint relief. A
hopeless misuse of lead,
18, 19, 20, 21, and
four years. A fat man
with a gunny
sack and a stick
with a nail on
the end
takes care
of the
trash.

Bob Grunst

QUESTIONS

A student told me he came into political science class thinking about something that got to him last week in class. He said to himself, "*I begin to see now, because George is having trouble with the traffic court and can't find a way of introducing his evidence without taking the case to a jury trial—that's not quite what we were discussing last week but it's related, and I'd like to ask about that—*" and the professor is saying,

"Now let's discuss what we were talking about last week. I'd like to go on to the second point, which was 'What is the traffic court's position in the administrative hierarchy?' "

The student was ready to make his point. *Second* point?

"Then the *third* point—"

The student was primed to say something of value to him and the other students, perhaps taking them beyond the level the teacher was working at. But no opportunity

"No one has anything to say about this third point? George, you've been a good student in this class. At least you could say something about the third point, couldn't you?"

The British actor Robert Morley once said on Jack Paar's television program, "School is all wrong. They ask you what you don't know, not what you know. When I took the test in sixth grade, 'Where is Cape Fear?' I said I didn't know but that I could give the names of the Twelve Apostles and I did."

THE RIGHT ANSWER

From a tape made in a Third Way class:

Something was on my mind about what you said once before about the matter of a teacher asking questions in a classroom. At first I probably agreed, I mean, what can he do if he can't ask questions? But when he asks a question, a specific question, he usually has a specific answer in mind and nine chances out of ten a specific way to get to that answer. Where if— this is true, though, if you really think about it—in this sense you really kill the creativity, because there must be a hundred thousand ways to reach one answer, even if you do have a definite answer in mind.

Real questions

At my university several years ago Martin Luther King, Jr., and Governor Ross Barnett of Mississippi spoke in the same year. Dr. King's appearance was notable for the small crowd it drew, and Governor Barnett's for the uproar it created. Today I thought that a record in writing in the yearbook of something of what each man said and did would now be valuable to alumni. Instead of making the year memorable, most college annuals strip it of its particularity. If the English professors had done their job, a yearbook editor might have printed this kind of comment. It was written by a student of mine in her journal. It records that in 1967 there was a war on:

M left this morning. I won't see him for more than a year unless he comes home in a coffin. I have a lot of regrets now. I wish we had gotten married when he was home instead of being so practical and waiting. I'm sorry for all the little arguments we had; they seem unimportant now. And, I never appreciated him enough; he was always the patient understanding one and I was the typical nag.

We have known for a long time that he would have to go, but I refused to really think about it. Now every news story and photograph of the war that I've seen flashes through my mind. The torture of prisoners, the weekly count of casualties, the hopelessness of jungle fighting. If I believed in this war, it wouldn't be as hard to bear. But the only certainty I have is M, and he left this morning.

The passage would have to be printed in the yearbook without the name of the writer. She has real questions about war. She would make a good student of history. She might ask why the War of Roses? Were young men coerced into participating in it?

The university need not devise devious ways of engaging students in the problems of this world. They live in it.

TEACHING DEVICE

At my university several years ago the vice-president for academic affairs sent round a note saying that many professors were de-emphasizing tests and that he saw no reason why anyone had to give finals if he didn't want to. Ever since then I have given no tests of any kind. My students' work is improving.

WHAT THE TEACHER WANTS

From a taped class discussion:

Last week in my German class we were reading Kafka's "Metamorphosis" in German, you know, and then we read a little about what Kafka thought the cover of the book should be, and it tells about how this Gregor gets to be an insect and somebody suggested you should put an insect on the top of the book and Kafka refused that because he thought then, you know, nobody would think any more what it should be like. They would have a fixed picture there, and it tells about how he is against the world, or the world is against him and his family, and then the teacher asked what would you suggest to be put on the cover, and I thought that maybe you should put a door there like suggesting it would be separating. And then a girl, well, she asked so many times and finally somebody said, "Well, a door," and I felt so let down because it was my brilliant idea and somebody came to tell that one, and the teacher was so happy and said, "Well, where did you get that idea? That's exactly what Kafka said, what he was thinking of putting on that cover," and I thought, "You know, if I had just told, that would have been just the answer the teacher wanted in order to do really good."

You know that's really funny because you kinda think what the teacher wants and I wasn't sure she wanted that so I didn't say it, and that's the answer. And I shouldn't have held back. You shouldn't, but I can't gear myself out of it.

EVALUATING THE PROFESSORS

Departments in universities tremble when time comes for promotion and tenure to be awarded teachers because the chairman and his advisors—usually the full professors who have tenure and the highest rank—have no notion of how good or bad their colleagues are as teachers.

Every few years they feel guilty about acting upon gossip and prejudice and chance meetings in the hall. They debate whether to make visitations to classrooms to see the teachers in action. "But that's not fair," some say, "maybe you'll hit him on a bad day."

Sometimes the committee looks at evaluations of the teachers written by students. But they aren't of much help because almost every teacher comes out the same way. "He wears a brown suit every day." "His assignments are too long." About two percent in each class say: "He's one of the best teachers I've ever had."

Since the day we killed Engfish I have been discovering that the professor should be tested by the performance of his students. Since most teachers don't improve that performance, the students have nothing valuable to say in evaluations. They could say, " a failure," but they seldom realize that is the truth because most of their professors are failures.

REAL EVALUATION

A senior student came into my office to tell me how he looks forward to getting out of school so he can once again read with pleasure. He should have put that down in his teacher evaluation.

NO DISCUSSION

Several years ago given the chance to teach the introductory Shakespeare course, I vowed it would not be like one I took at Oberlin College as an undergraduate, where we listened to rapid-fire lectures that covered the works, every single one Shakespeare wrote

I was given a class of forty-four students, a number that implies the course will be taught by lecture. I wanted my students to talk and not just answer questions. Most of them didn't care to say a word. They sat there in rows looking at the backs of students in front of them and couldn't get up nerve enough to throw their words over all those heads to me. Those few who said anything usually spoke Engfish.

After a few days I decided I would have to loosen up what I said if I were to get any honest statement from students. I began occasionally walking to the window and letting myself view a person or object outside that illustrated what I was talking about in Shakespeare. I began to talk better than ever before. More metaphors came to me and they were fresher and more apt than usual. I impressed myself. At the end of the semester two students said they found the course more lively than most.

It was the usual worthless student evaluation, but I had not the objectivity to see that.

A LITTLE DISCUSSION

In that Shakespeare class I had no trouble getting the students to find their own voices in papers they wrote. In the second or third paper, almost all of them abandoned Engfish and began writing like human beings. But they didn't want to talk in class.

One day I broke them into groups of four and said, "Go somewhere in the building and talk about what you think of Hamlet the man." They returned in thirty minutes and we had the best discussion I had ever heard in a literature class. With no cue from me, two groups squared off and let fly. Soon most of the students were saying something that counted for them. And it counted for me.

SOCRATIC

A couple of years ago I attended a general education conference where a young leader of a new school at the University of Chicago told of his supposedly radical methods of teaching. He had found the Socratic method. At first he won me because he admitted Socratic questions are not questions at all, but subterfuges. The teacher asks a question and pretends not to know the answer. "It's a pulling," said the speaker, "like grabbing the ring in the bull's nose, intended to jerk and shock and be somewhat painful. You've got to shake these middle-class kids up. In fact, that's your central duty, to confuse them and make them think for the first time."

I became ill listening to that man. He was saying meet students at their weakness, confuse them, and make them weaker. Then spring your stuff on them. If he were to turn that round to himself—to ask students to question him about the things he knew least about, how would he feel? How would he learn?

PERSONAL CONFERENCE

Since the day we killed Engfish, I have stopped encouraging students to come to my office for "personal conferences." In the professor's office the student knows where he is—the place one goes to when he has done badly. There he is seldom going to speak truths. And so the professor does all the talking; or he asks questions, and gets *his* answers.

From kindergarten through graduate school the American school system is built upon the fact of students talking and writing for Teacher. Not with other students, and him, but to him and for him.

A BIG DISCUSSION

Now, after my students have read a play by Shakespeare, I let them point themselves the way their minds have traveled. Here is a transcript of a taped class discussion:

Professor: What's this man King Lear like? What do you think of him? (One girl registered disgust audibly.) Miss Kendall doesn't like him, so I won't let her talk. What do the rest of you think of him? Just your frank, honest opinion, and if you don't like him, don't say anything."

(Silence, then laughter.)

No, you can talk, Miss Kendall. What do you think of him?

Kendall: *I don't like him.*

Professor: All right, good. Why not?

Kendall: *Uh, he lets his daughters push him around, and, of course, I don't like his daughters either. They're kind of ungrateful—not too nice. That's mildly putting it.* (Laughter in the class)

Crowell: *It just seems like he's lost something, a great perspective. This one daughter, well, she sort of told the truth and the other two lied, and he, well, seemed really old and he'd lost, you know, the truth, and he couldn't see that his other two daughters were just flattering him, and he seemed sort of senile and it seemed sort of sad. To me, at least, it seemed that when he was older he couldn't realize. It wasn't that I didn't like him. I just felt sorry for him.*

Tenk: *I felt sorry for him because he reminded me of my grandmother when she was still living. Well, really. Maybe he's got hardening of the arteries or something. Feel sorry for him, poor old man, he just wanted love and security in his old age and he wasn't getting it.*

Roarke: *I felt even kind of pathetic. I could see that once there was a spirit there and it had really gotten broken by circumstances and he was just such an idealistic person that he didn't want to face things even when they were brought before him. Like, you know, he had to have all of his guards with him to go with him from house to house. That amount, you know, just so he could retain some of his kingliness type of thing. I realize this was sort of a security thing he needed so he could build up—*

Professor: His security blanket was a hundred retainers. (Laughter.)

Roarke: *Yeah, it was kind of a big one.* (Laughter.)

Winslow (Married woman in early thirties): *I just don't know why, but I've gotten—possibly because of a birthday just past—but I've gotten a picture of King Lear in more middle age. I don't know. I guess it's the idea of this security business. You've passed the point of being able to choose your occupation and do the things you could when you're making your decision of what you want to be. So he's reached the point where he's far from retirement and yet close enough* (sigh) *so he can't* (sigh), *oh, he can't give up the things he's already gotten. And so as a result, as he gets old in the play, he achieves the wisdom that comes with old age. I don't think he's senile. I think he's just— he's got his eyes on too many other things. He's been fooled by the other sisters. I think this is a middle-aged thing rather than older.*

Professor: The way it starts out—

Roarke: *No, I think sometimes—*

Professor: "The wisdom that comes with age." You better watch out. That's not a very popular thing to say these days.

(Smile from Roarke and small laughter among other students.)

Roarke: *No, I think because the older people aren't encumbered by all these other values, they can see things in other people that other people can't see. They can see sometimes things a little bit differently—sometimes wrong, but sometimes right.*

Professor: You don't mean that wisdom necessarily comes to all older people?

Roarke: *No, I didn't mean that. But sometimes it comes because they're unencumbered with the security values that the younger people have.*

(Twenty-second silence.)

Farr: *It seems like this fear of losing security or desire for security makes him too literal minded, uh, like when he asks his daughters so much to love him and treats them accordingly. There's no attempt to decipher any hidden motives behind their answers and in his reaction throughout the play after that it seemed to be—there's not great inner debate about what a person's intentions really are. He takes it at face value and goes into a rage, or whatever.*

Professor: Do you think he takes things at face value so much that this is a fault of the play—that he seems unbelievable? It's a pretty wild thing he does at the opening, isn't it? He tosses off his best daughter and gives his wealth to the two people who turn out to be so awful?

Crowell: *I think that's possible, because when you love somebody, you know, when you're really close, you, uh, believe them, so you do, and you don't usually question the motives. When the one daughter was just whipping out with the line "I love you as much as—" he was giving her a chance. He was saying, "Lookit, I'm giving you a warning, you know, if you don't shape up with this speech, I'm going to kick you out." And so he was trying to make her understand that for him this was necessary and she was just herself, you know, she couldn't still be herself and do what her sisters were doing.*

Professor: Sounds like a 1968 girl to me— not going to be deferential to the old pot. (Laughter.)

Brown: *I think that that was ungrateful because that happened in my family. My grandfather got very old and very senile. And it was—people who had been very close to him, and he had a great affection for, just switched. And those that were actually, you know, kind of immoral, all of a sudden thought they were much better. He didn't realize that people who were really close to him, even though he was an old grouch, used to love him. And the other people only came around every two months or so, and fortunately now, he's gone back to them. And it just seemed very realistic to me that this daughter did really love him more than others but she wasn't going to say things she didn't want to.*

Professor: It's interesting that you saw something like that in—

Howell: *I think it's interesting what has been brought out about Cordelia. Actually she might have been acting selfishly in a way. I had never looked at it in that light before—that in a way if he really was old and senile, why couldn't she just give in a little to him a little bit I didn't see that at the beginning, but it is another way of looking at it.*

Professor: Why couldn't she have said something—"I'll tell you later more," or anything, but no, sort of "I love you as much as anybody should and you take it or leave it." No attempt to understand him at that point at all. Now it would be interesting, I think, to look at Cordelia's part in the play and see if you think she's headstrong or selfish in any way later, even though she's made out to have been the one loyal daughter. Is she maybe complicated, like Shakespeare's people usually are? She loved her father, but she's still got some independence and she goes a little far in this case, and it gets her all *wrecked up*, as the kids say in my house.

Tenk: *That's what I couldn't understand—why she could not tell him what he wanted her to, when he was really that old. Because I know my grandmother's in a nursing home and there's some people out there that really don't know what time of day it is, or whether it's night or day. They ask, "Are you Ethel?" and you say "Yes," and they're perfectly happy, and you walk away, you know, and you would want to tell them what they want to hear.*

Crowell: *But I could see Cordelia, if you had two sisters who just gushed and made you ill to your stomach—I could see—I have a feeling for him, but I'm just not going to be like that because it was such a falsehood, because it would be like a falsehood for you to do the same thing.*

Professor: Maybe we're in another one of those situations where given these people—they're going to, you know, rub against each other instead of do what we would think is nice and rational and intelligent. Certainly isn't rational, but how often do we proceed with equanimity and rationality and justice for all? I don't at least not while I'm home (Laughter.) Wow! That's where they were—home. That wonderful place. Reminds me of that article I was reading in *Look* magazine about marriages. You ought to look at it, about the thing they called home, where everybody is tied up in this little tiny place out of communication with the rest of the world, having their difficulties rubbing up against each other. .

(At this point the tape ran out.)

In that discussion, my students performed as I wanted them to. They brought their own experience to their reading but they did not let it distort Shakespeare's characters. They learned from each other, pushing down several levels below the surface on which they began. They interrupted me and each other, but usually at exquisitely intuited moments, when the speaker had run out of gas, or was himself interrupting a valuable flow of their remarks. The tone of their voices and their laughter (which I cannot give here) was bright and positive, not vicious and self-righteous.

These conversing students did not sound like intellectuals—my colleagues and I at a cocktail hour or staff meeting, each showing off his knowledge for a moment, then going silent to hone his knife while someone else talks. On the contrary, the students seemed intellectually curious.

Critics

In that Shakespeare class I asked the students to read some of the essays by established critics which followed one of the plays in our paperbound editions and to say why they agreed or disagreed with them on a point or two. In her journal, Jo Ann Blain wrote:

All of the critics we read this week had good things to say, and I could criticize very few of them for their style of writing. But I have become accustomed to listening to ideas on the play, so it seems a little hard to have to read something that doesn't seem as emotional at first glance as the girl across the room who feels that her honor is at stake along with that of King Richard.

"Over the last year the mean scores of students taking the Minnesota-Thuringer Test changed plus or minus one hundredths of a percent."

Performance

DRAMA

My Shakespeare students didn't know how to read drama as if it were primarily two persons talking to each other with tension—responding, confronting, or not responding in a significant way. So I asked each student to write a one-page drama in which persons with real voices said real things that counted for them, and the whole added up in some way. They did this. I was astonished, and so were they. Some of the little plays had to be published in a literary supplement to the campus newspaper, and dozens had to be posted on a bulletin board in the corridor of the building where I held class. Knots of students from other classes and departments collected around the posted papers.

I can remember months later many of the dramas—the one about the girl introducing her new roommate to her old roommate now clerking in a department store and pregnant with illegitimate child, the one about the boy who angrily moved out of the dorm because he had to live three students in a room and joyously found freedom in a town apartment where he was living three in a room, the one about the young man arguing in a bar with his friend about his inability to decide what to do about the draft—he thought the war immoral but was not a pacifist.

None of the dramas have been sustained, complex artistic works. But they exhibit many of the devices employed by Shakespeare and other professionals—irony, interruption, play on words, alliteration, metaphor, careful and accurate differentiation of dialects, change of voice within one man's speech as he moves into different situations, etc. Whether or not they succeed as dramatic sketches, these one-page workouts help students read Shakespeare as a playwright and appreciate his range and command. I do not grade them and no one seems disappointed.

One of these dramatic dialogues, a little longer than usual, comprises the next entry in this journal.

WITHHOLD

(At registration a student waits in line, three alternate schedules written on a piece of notebook paper, her student ID and No. 3 card in one hand and two ball point pens in the other. She approaches the table.)

Clerk (without expression): Student ID please. (The student hands the piece of plastic to her.) 943057. (She flips through the file drawer.) Your cards are on a financial withhold.

Student: Financial withhold?

Clerk: You must have some kind of a financial obligation to the University. Check with the man in the brown suit at Table 23.

Student: Where's that?

Clerk: On the other side of the field house, third table from the end. Next.

Student (dubiously): Thank you. (She walks hurriedly to Table 23, where she gets in a line of only twelve people. She approaches the table, slightly impatient.) They told me over there that I had a financial withhold on my cards. I don't owe any money.

Administrator: You must. All of the financial dealings of the University are programmed through a computer. This eliminates the possibility of human error. Who are you?

Student: Jane Alice McRoy.

Administrator: No, no—your student number. I need your student number.

Student: 943057.

Administrator: Our records show you paid the University an extra dollar on last term's room payment.

Student: So?

Administrator: So you have to clear this up before you are allowed to register. You go to the Ad Building, the housing director's office, and they will see that you receive a check.

Student: That's all right, they can have the dollar, I just want to register. Can you give me an OK to register?

Administrator: I'm sorry. You'll have to clear this up first.

Student: I can't—it'll take all afternoon. They've already let in the next registration group. I've got to get in there before all the classes close! This is my last semester and I have to have my classes!

Administrator: Don't get snippy, young lady. Just do as you're told. (Turns away.)

Student: Wait a minute! I'll make the contribution of a dollar to the University. I'm sure they can use it.

Administrator: The sooner you go to the Ad Building, the sooner you will be able to register. (The student turns to go, somewhat dejected.) Wait a minute! You forgot your No. 3 card. You'll need it at the Ad Building. (The student takes the card and folds it neatly to put in her pocket.) Don't fold it! Can't you read? It says "Do not fold, bend, or mutilate" If it is folded, it will not be accepted.

(As the student walks away, she begins to fold her card in such a way that by the time she reaches the door, it is neatly compacted into a 1" x 1" square. She nonchalantly flips it into a waste basket along with a piece of notebook paper. She looks around quickly, gives the waste basket a swift kick, crams her hands in her pocket, and walks slowly out of the field house.)

Jan Whitmore

STUDENTS' CONTEMPT

A girl who early in my Shakespeare course had turned in a sharp paper asked to talk to me after class. In an empty room she embarrassedly but determinedly told me that in the small college from which she had transferred she had studied under a teacher who admired me, that she had a great deal of respect for me, but she couldn't stand the class because it didn't offer any "*hard-core scholarship.*" She said, "*I don't want to listen to some sorority chick telling what she said to a friend in the cafeteria line.*" She was referring to a student-written dramatic dialogue that had been read in our class.

Hard-core. I thought of how the epithet has sounded to me on the tongues of the narrow-minded and ignorant. I have heard them talking of "hard-core pornography" and "hard-core communists," all the while licking their lips as if evil tasted delicious.

Writing this entry, I was interrupted by dinner; and before I got back to it, I read in a paper that the statewide commander of the National Guard had defended the spraying of military gas by helicopter on the university campus in Berkeley, California, where hospital patients and mothers watching children at a swimming pool were disturbed and frightened. He said that the "discomfort and inconvenience to innocent bystanders . . . is an inescapable by-product of combatting terrorists, anarchists, and *hard-core* militants on the streets and on the campus."

In a way I don't blame any of these users of the epithet *hard-core*. The commander didn't know his enemies and naturally he wasn't seeing them at their best. The girl in my class had reason for suspecting her fellow students. In First or Second Way classes, they had probably either acted like automatons or let their tongues spin loose on trivial reels. But for the moment, her comment challenged me. Maybe I was being soft on my students, overrating what they said and wrote in that class. No. I had taped many of their discussions and been excited listening a second time. And so had my wife, an unsentimental critic of my students. This girl was the rare student who feels close to her professors, who talks with them before and after class and is invited to their homes for tea. She had learned her contempt from masters.

ONCE AGAIN

When I saw an advertisement for a new book called *A Writer Teaches Writing*, I sent for it, hoping it might help the cause of the New English.

In it, I came upon this sentence: "No teacher will convert all the hard-core anti-writers."

DESPISING

I continued reading and was surprised to find that on point after point the author was trying to liberate teachers. In almost every respect he was a New English teacher. The methods he advocated showed respect for students. He said they should write first out of their own experience, that they be given both the freedom and discipline that a professional works with. He cared about what students said, asked for truths, put punctuation and spelling last —where they belong. Like me in my early days of teaching, he found that the red correction marks in the margins of themes worsened rather than helped the writing. Sometimes he wrote an assigned paper along with his students, and accepted their criticism of it. And yet he seemed ambivalent toward them. He said:

> We have equality of opportunity, but, thank God, not a bland equality of accomplishment . . . when we find someone who has not spoken before discovering his own voice, it is the most satisfying thing that can happen to a teacher. It's worth all the disappointments, all the defeats, for that *one* victory. [My italics.]

BLAND ACCOMPLISHMENT

I found myself getting angry at this teacher. But when I cooled down, I had to accept his feelings as valid—if I was to live with my own past contempt for students. Both of us had reason to look down on students. They had written contemptibly—evasively, pretentiously, dully.

This professional writer did not yet see that the whole educational system tells the student to write Engfish and that the writing of it fulfills not the explicit, large demands of most teachers, which are for truth and originality and communication; but the implicit demands, which are for perfect mechanics, proper form, and sterilized language.

And he did not realize that a teacher who believes only one or two of the students in each of his classes are capable of doing fine work will in subtle ways communicate that lack of faith. Then his exhortations and promises ring false. They reach the student's unconscious finally as discouragement.

BE SPECIFIC

Occasionally in New English classes I have found one or two students in the first few weeks who could not break free of Engfish. Once or twice I have succumbed and said, "Just put down a bunch of telling facts." Usually the advice had not worked, and I had to ask them to continue free writing for several more weeks while the other students moved on to more planned and crystallized papers.

Last semester I risked telling an inhibited student flatly that she must try a paper in which she stated no opinion, just facts. Here is the paper she turned in:

Every time I try to speak of my father I find words like gentle, sweet, funny, or shy popping up, and they are useless, meaningless. "Tell what your father did, what he said," you said, and I am stuck. How do I make a story from the things my father did?

I will tell you what he did.

My father walked to the far side of our pasture, found a cow with her newborn calf, and carried the calf home in his arms.

My father was rarely seen without at least two small children on or around him. He gave them horseback rides, told them funny stories, and lifted them atop a cow named Blackie, who didn't mind being used for a horse—his own children—until one by one all six of them grew too old for that sort of nonsense, then the young nieces and nephews, and next, last, the neighbor's children.

My dad followed me upstairs after he punished me once and said he was sorry and rubbed my back until I didn't cry any more.

He raised and cared for twenty-five pure-bred Jersey cows, and he sang while he worked away his life and was poorer than any other farmer in the county.

My dad made a huge bowl of popcorn and spent countless hours reading Agatha Christie murder mysteries in bed as he munched.

Because he was an incurable dreamer, he straightened out the family's financial crises only on paper, by selling cows which in reality he could not bear to lose because he loved them.

When he was forty-seven years old my dad found out that he had a very serious heart condition, and he never went across the road to the barn again, but sat silent before the pot-bellied stove in our kitchen and puffed on a pipe. Every day he made tea and dry jokes for his wife and children and visitors.

When he felt stronger, he was sent to be rehabilitated in Waterloo, Iowa. On a bitter, cold day in January, 1959, he died in his sleep. He did not live to see his cows taken away that morning by the man who had bought them.

DEWEY'S GHOST

The author of *A Writer Teaches Writing* acknowledges the help of at least forty teachers who followed his program, yet he presents as samples of student work only two or three fairly strong papers and a number of poor and mediocre ones.

Good theory without good results. I fear it. Students may suffer a backlash from teachers who came so close to liberating them. This has happened before in the misapplication of the educational theories of John Dewey, who formulated all the right principles and illuminated the terrifying weaknesses of American education. To little avail.

In *School and Society*, first published in 1899, he described the nature and causes of Engfish:

> Think of the absurdity of having to teach language as a thing by itself. If there is anything the child will do before he goes to school, it is to talk of the things that interest him. But when there are no vital interests appealed to in the school, when language is used simply for the repetition of lessons, it is not surprising that one of the chief difficulties of school work has come to be instruction in the mother-tongue. Since the language taught is unnatural, not growing out of the real desire to communicate vital impressions and convictions, the freedom of children in its use gradually disappears, until finally the high-school teacher has to invent all kinds of devices to assist in getting any spontaneous and full use of speech. Moreover, when the language instinct is appealed to in a social way, there is a continual contact with reality. The result is that the child always has something in his mind to talk about, he has something to say; he has a thought to express, and a thought is not a thought unless it is one's own. In the traditional method, the child must say something that he has merely learned. There is all the difference in the world between having something to say and having to say something.

But Dewey's insight was not applied in a way that freed many American children to use their own voices in the classroom.

Expository

John Dewey was a seer. He predicted the invention of "all kinds of devices to assist in getting any spontaneous and full use of speech." Like filling in the columns under "Sensory Details" in the exercise I forced on my Michigan State students.

Since Dewey died, teachers have invented dozens of ingenious and essentially tyrannical devices of this kind. In the October, 1963, issue of *College English,* a professors' journal, two instructors at the University of Nebraska introduced what they jokingly but accurately called "A Slide-Rule Composition Course,' in which they taught "the student to use language in ways that neither he nor anybody else uses it in speech." They added, "This is clear and unobjectionable." They asked the student

> to complete ten to fifteen inductive projects and to write four to ten pages about each project. He begins by investigating purely formal features, such as sentence length, paragraph length, and the location of expansion within sentences. . .

Shades of Percival! I'm sure these teachers did not intend to teach Engfish, but their push was to remove talk from school writing, when in most classes that is exactly what should be put back into it. These teachers were afraid of subjectivity. It is frightening at times, but only when one is struggling with both subjectivity and objectivity is he apt to write live and telling sentences.

They said their aim in the freshman course was to teach expository writing. ***Expository.*** Horrible academic word. Most students never heard it before. Sounds to them like something that must be purchased in drug stores.

SOURCES

Thinking about teachers' ability to contrive what should come naturally for students reminded me of a weird movement that occurred in the 1950's. English professors had long been enraged at students for writing term papers on euthanasia and the Civil War by stealing library books or cutting out passages from magazines when they found materials were short in the library. As usual, the students were reading the cues clearly—they looked to the subjects students had chosen in the past and decided they were what Teacher wanted. So the range of subjects continually decreased. The true and naturally varied interests of the students never became manifest. A few students stole or plagiarized materials wholesale; most students faithfully performed the laborious job of cramming their long and empty papers with dull, interminable quotations ("You must have at least fifteen citations from books and ten from magazines") from trustworthy and untrustworthy sources senselessly scrambled together. At that time no one suspected that cutting up library books and magazines might be a communication from students to teachers like that of breaking windows.

The patience of everyone was running out. To save university libraries from large-scale mutilation, a professor at Ohio University put together a casebook which provided the raw materials for writing a paper on John Brown's raid—contemporary newspaper and magazine reports, comments on Brown by famous figures, military reports, a map, etc. The textbook was called *Incident at Harper's Ferry,* "primary source materials for teaching the theory and technique of the investigative essay." It is one of the most exciting, dramatic books I have ever read, among the most treasured in my library.

But the design of the casebook spoke differently to the student: it told him once again that he did not possess a curiosity about anything worthwhile, that he lacked the basic human compulsion to pursue a significant investigation. The casebook denied him the thrill of tracking things down while he was supposedly at that very task.

But again, the teacher had good reason to invent such a device. His students had never shown intellectual curiosity in the classroom and had demonstrated incredible, malicious irresponsibility in the library.

The new method for getting better term papers didn't work well, but the casebook manifested a professors' dream. Each book could center on a specific event or problem in the social, political, or artistic world. The scholar could make a book out of his Ph.D. thesis or his special interest at the moment. In less than ten years 132 casebooks appeared, all issued by reputable publishers. I found most of them fascinating. When I was editor of *College Composition and Communication,* I published an annotated bibli ography of them prepared by a professor who was also fascinated by them (May 1962, May 1963).

These were unusual scholarly publications. Some, like those on Ezra Pound and "Mark Twain's Wound," were beyond most freshmen, but all took up significant controversies. They presented original and contemporary reports and opinions rather than straining the materials through a scholar's small sieve. The fruit and seeds and trash of the time could be touched by the untrained reader. They are valuable books. They carry a sense of reality and make learning fun. They should be reprinted without the instructions to term-paper-writing students, both as trade books for the general public and texts for the schools.

But with these mind-opening books the professors once again managed to insult their students.

Respecting one's work

Freedom is nothing unless it leads to valuable thoughts, conversations, objects, writing. And valuable to others as well as the person who produces them. The psychology is simple, as Erich Fromm pointed out long ago. If others do not respect our work, then we cannot respect it. And if we do not respect it, it will not be such that others respect it. There is a discipline involved here that takes one down to the core of being individually and socially human.

Beginners

Unlike most English teachers, the author of *A Writer Teaches Writing* knows the fundamentals. He tells the would-be writer to

> Be aware—use all of your senses, read, listen, be receptive to new ideas.

> Be informed—accumulate a body of knowledge.
> Be concerned.

These are sounder instructions than the requirement that every paragraph should have a topic sentence and the thesis should be stated explicitly at the beginning of the theme.

But being concerned involves something more than obeying instructions. The author of every good piece of writing was concerned. And Engfish students are not concerned, except about grades. But their apathy has been brought about by the teacher, not by themselves; and so the instruction is insulting—no, even worse, degrading. It comes to their ears like the words of an overseer who tells his slaves, "You should be thankful for the chance to witness this whipping. It will show you what evil befalls the slave who does not take an interest in his work."

The author of *A Writer Teaches Writing* forgets that the beginning writer in college or high school is not a beginning human being. He has already acquired a body of knowledge or he would not be alive. He is concerned about many things, not always those which fascinate the teacher. The author of this book knows that and even says it in several places, but he cannot refrain from presenting these condescending instructions. On page 138 he says:

> Fear of a poor grade is not a good motivation, and undeserved A's in writing presented to students who are articulate in comparison with the boobs they sit with in a given classroom do positive harm to the student who thinks he knows how to write when he doesn't.

THE BOOBS ARE THE TEACHERS

"Develop a sense of irony—perspective, humor," says the author of *A Writer Teaches Writing*. The instruction seems laughable to me today. Yet only a few years ago teaching Honors students at Michigan State I was telling them to write a satire, explaining the mode brilliantly I thought, and receiving nothing but awkward, heavy-handed papers.

Now I get humorous and biting papers frequently, almost always from students who have not been directed exactly what or how to write.

I believe the assignment was "Write something about childhood" when Mrs. Naomi Yuk turned in this letter which she thought her son's teacher should read:

Dear Mrs. Grint:

My son Robert is in your music class. As you know, he left his music book on the school bus last Friday. Robert has searched the bus, asked the drivers, the principal, the janitor, his teacher, even the school cook—without success.

You told him you could not understand how a nine-year-old boy could be so careless, irresponsible, and ungrateful; and strongly suggested that he lacked proper home training.

Robert is careless and irresponsible, and most of the time I wouldn't change him if I knew how. He's careless and irresponsible, Mrs. Grint, about your values and mine, not his. Robert's world consists of baseball, frogs, snakes, bubble gum, and more baseball. He takes his mitt to school every day and doesn't lose it. He spends hours down at the pond collecting frogs and snakes.

Ungrateful! Why should he be grateful to you for driving out every natural musical desire he has ever had? Sending that damn book home to be covered is a case in point. You've made it a sin for a child to have an uncovered book in your class. You shout at your students, humiliate them before their friends if they sing a wrong note, or sing too loud or not loud enough. If their attention wanders, you assign them an extra report on Bach or Mozart.

It is true, as the school administration points out, that your students learn music—music theory, music history, and music antagonism. I'm sorry for your students, Mrs. Grint. They've been cheated. They've had to pay too high a price for learning to sing on pitch. I'm sorry for you too. You've paid too much for the covers on those music books.

A clear perspective, and a good bit of ironic humor.

MARIE'S HEART

One of my colleagues said to me, "These kids in our classes aren't Faulkners or Shakespeares. Under your writing program they could easily get the idea they are."

I had to answer, "No, not easily. Not at all."

When freshman Marie Pineau wrote,

I leaned against the washer and as it began its cycle, my entire body pulsated with it. It was as if I were holding my heart in my hand, and I was terribly excited. Then suddenly the washer stopped.

I thought, "Don't let Marie's heart stop. She's too much alive." To my colleagues I point out that she has written a consistent and generating metaphor, like many of Shakespeare's best. But she has not written *Hamlet*. Or even one of Hamlet's soliloquies. It is my job and Marie's to see likenesses and differences. The better writer she becomes, the more of Shakespeare's excellences she is apt to perceive. Writing at times like a great writer will not hurt her.

PROSY

Today I told a girl her page of prose was trying to be a poem It was concentrated, sensuous, but *complete* in its small compass.

"Why don't you try to make it into a poem?"

She beamed, pleased that I thought it worth that form. "*O.K.*," She spoke enthusiastically, then walked toward the door There she turned back and said, "*But I don't know the first thing about writing poetry.*"

She was a university senior who had majored in English, studied poems for at least six years, heard them analyzed in lectures, read close examinations of them in critical articles; and she had no idea of what was in them or how they were made up.

CAMPUS POETRY

That was a smart girl who knew she didn't know how to write a poem. Most English majors think they know and don't. I take an example from a college literary magazine that is uncopyrighted and here unidentified, so as not to embarrass its editors or the author.

Let me exist in the hell of the mind,
Let me sleep naked in beds of hot coals,
Let me drink the acid of gossip,
Suck in the airs of persecution,
Laugh at the beatings of ignorance.

But let me not lose love,
For then all pain will cease—
All joy will cease.

Death is no longer a fear
For it holds salvation of pain,
Salvation of joy.

Let me cry, let me pain,
For love yet thrives on pain.
For in pain life is lived.

Unaware, this writer had been Engfishified.

STAYING AFTER SCHOOL

Patti Shirley came to Advanced Writing class having missed several sessions—and without any writing to turn in. I was angry because I had told the class they would have to submit something that day, if only a page of free writing.

"*I don't have it,*" she said.

"Then sit down right now and in the next twenty minutes fill at least a page and bring it to my office," I said. I left the room feeling alternately justified and cruel.

A knock at the door, Patti entered, and laid a yellow sheet on my desk. "*I was looking out the window,*" she said, "*at the fountain in the plaza—and I just wrote this off. It's a poem. I don't know—*"

"All right," I said. "Thanks. It's a piece of writing. It will do."

She left and I couldn't resist picking up the paper right away.

PATTI'S POEM

A friend
alive last month
is
today,
I'm told,
a dead box of rocks
        en route
    from Saigon.

Outside the
smoke filmed
    window
a boy balances
    on the edge of the fountain,
    dirty blue paint & empty.

            Only
        last spring
    it was my ocean.

POETRY ALL OVER THE CAMPUS

The sign in the Student Union for the Snow Carnival consisted of one gigantic letter of the words THINK SNOW in each window. They were put up there two weeks before the carnival. On the day it was to start, and still no snow, the sign was changed to THINK NOW; two days later, to THINK. The changes were accomplished simply by removing letters. The carnival date arrived without snow, and on that day the sign again displayed two words: THINK NO. The word play of the students had saved the event from being pure dismal.

In the Britton Hall dormitory a handlettered sign appeared one day in the window: "This Is National Conserve Your Virginity Week."

I asked my students to bring to class materials for poetry that they themselves had invented and also to record in their journals the exquisite fact of their environment. Sue Ptacek noted that a man daily entered the all-girls' dorm carrying a bag marked "Domestic Mail."

One boy reported that the minister's daughter had got pregnant last summer at church camp.

Sharon Williams found a dead bird with its mangled wing held in place by "magic transparent tape."

Cathy Todd noted that when visiting high school students crowded the University Student Union, a friend said to her, "Are these all high school kids? I wish the bell would ring."

Lorna Vest reported that in Ann Arbor she saw

A pimply-faced, dirty, barefooted, greasy, stringy haired girl smoking a cigarette and eating a peanut butter and jelly sandwich riding a crowded elevator at the University of Michigan while reading How to Win Friends and Influence People.

THE INHUMANITIES

While my students were recording such wild and lovely stuff, I found on the table in my seminar room a piece of note paper carrying these words handwritten in red ink:

> 10:35: Call on students to correct the incorrect examples 9-14.

10:45: Remind students to note tonight's assignment and ask if there are any questions.

10:50: Have students clear their desks, take out pencil & paper and answer the quiz questions.

10:56: Collect quiz papers and read off correct answers.

11:00: Dismiss.

I don't know whether these sentences had been dictated by a teacher, copied from a textbook, or made up by a student asked to prepare a lesson plan; but none of those reasons could excuse such deadliness to me.

FABULOUS

Reading *Walden*, I came upon this passage:

> Shams and delusions are esteemed for soundest truth, while reality is fabulous. If men would steadily observe realities only, and not allow themselves to be deluded, life, to compare it with such things as we know, would be like a fairy tale and the Arabian Nights' Entertainments.

Next day I went to class and ordered the students to spend a weekend recording *fabulous realities*. They came rolling in and have ever since that day:

1. *An elderly, sparse man who makes a career out of auditing classes is sitting next to me taking notes on both sides of a paper. Now he turns it upside down and writes over his old notes.*
2. *A young lady's fifty-cent check to the Optimist Club bounced.*
3. *A man returned to his parked car to find its hood and fenders gashed and crumpled. On the dashboard he found a piece of folded paper. Written in a neat feminine hand, the note said: "I have just run into your car. There are people watching me. They think I am writing down my name and address. They are wrong."*
4. *A girl with a deep V in her blouse holding her books over it.*
5. *A pregnant woman had been collecting a twenty-four hour urine sample at home. An empty fifth of Scotch was the only bottle she had large enough to carry the urine in. She put the bottle in a paper sack and left for the doctor's office. On the way she stopped at a grocery store. Upon returning to her car, she noticed the paper sack containing the bottle was missing.*

"I don't know how
we can expect them to write.
They haven't had any significant
experiences. They aren't yet mature."

PERSONS

MALCOLM AGAIN

From California Malcolm sent me a letter apologizing for dropping out of my writing class without explanation, and describing his adventures:

It's a short time now that I've been here in Los Angeles, but I'm with a friend, and that helps because he's taken me from place to place that would've taken me by myself a long time to find and get myself into. Like in Claremont, a conservative town of several liberal colleges, there is the New School, which meets in the open house of a girl friendly-eyed named Tracy. I say open because the door was open and though Tracy and her little girl lived upstairs, the downstairs was like a hotel with the moving-in and-outs of people of styles galore. The idea was to provide a place to get together on a subject, like Contemporary Approaches to God, which I sat in on, and not be taken up with those bothers of structured school happenings like meeting three times a week for lectures and tests and homework. I mean the talk was personal and what was said was what was felt; you weren't concerned with obligating your questions to the professor only in an effort to look bright and get that A, which was what I saw happening at Western, even in the Good Doctor Macrorie's class, and why I got out of there. I think it was Harvey who said in an article to be printed in The Activist, *that when you drop out of school you learn about life, but you don't learn about anything else. Glad I was to see inclinations to life in this New School. They were mostly girls from an all-girl school there in Claremont, but there was me and a professor of Scripps College Religion Dept. We began on an abstract level of theology, talking about the importance and meaning and significance of Kierkegaard and Nietzsche and Buber, and then about how and why Heidegger lived alone in the woods with his dog, and then it became personal, as if that's what we were really there for. Tracy was trying to say what it was, why it was that she still believed, and I was sitting there and watching, thinking how alone people really are and how hungry we are for the personal.*

PERSONS

Peg Stevens, one of the students in my Advanced Writing class, wrote an account of her cheering-up visits to patients at the nearby mental hospital. Her last lines read:

Robert Lowell, Theodore Roethke, and Ezra Pound, twentieth century writers we students admire in class, have been in and out of institutions all their lives. We will fill the institutions. The girl down the hall who cries when her roommate suggests changes in her themes. The boy in Bigelow who is drunk by 4:00 p.m. The girl afraid to take Shakespeare but who wants to go to grad school at U. of M. Another girl who speaks to no one. We will be stuttering and slobbering where they are now. I went out for the last time this month.

My first reaction was that Miss Stevens had wrecked her fine case-history with a melodramatic ending. She or her classmates aren't going to be mental patients, I thought. But a year later, another girl wrote of her recent experience.

Can't stay here alone, not a healthy thing. I dragged my medicated body off the bed, stood it in front of a mirror, and then combed its hair. Almost 4:30, time to gather in the lounge for medication.

She had been there already and she was twenty.

High School Kids

A high school teacher at Kalamazoo Central heard about my writing program, instituted it in his creative writing courses, and soon was sending me work by his students that jolted my wife and me. I carry this paper always in my memory:

Her mother always made her clean the bird cage after school instead of letting her play like the rest of us. She had a fat little sister that always sounded like she was screeching when she talked. I quit 4H because her mother was the leader. Her bird finally died, but her mother still made her stay in. I was really shocked when I found out she was gonna have a baby. I can hardly remember her boy friend, I think he was in the band or something.

John Bennett, the teacher of that writer, now sends me several hundred writings a year that carry that sort of power. We publish a magazine of our students' writing every semester. Call it *Unduressed* to suggest what students can do when they are out from under the duress of writing Engfish. When the secretary in the English office read a copy of the magazine, she said to me, "You know it's funny, but I think the writing by the high school students is stronger than the writing by the college students."

Right. The high school kids haven't been schooled as many years in Engfish.

Schoolteachers

When I realized that high school students could get to truth faster than college students, I remembered that the young and middle-aged schoolteachers I had taught in a National Defense Education Act Institute in the summer of 1966 had taken longer than any of my other students to free themselves from the empty proprieties of Engfish. But eventually they produced some lively truths in that Institute classroom because they were persons, too.

One teacher wrote in her journal:

When I think of barnacles I laugh because if they were attached to my bottom I'd feel important—like the Queen Mary. Maybe I ought to think like this when I take a bath and slide across the porcelain ocean at the end of a narrow day.

JOURNAL ENTRY #1

Often when asked what is on their minds, students in my writing classes offer up the most recent Fabulous Reality they have witnessed. Sometimes they read it from their journals, sometimes speak it off the cuff. Kathy Wait read:

During the party some people were out on the sun deck talking. It was cold that night, so I closed the glass sliding door. Lou Anne, somewhat inebriated, decided to join the party inside, walked splat into the door, and bounced off. Rachel looked over at me and said, quite seriously, "I thought only birds did that.'

JOURNAL ENTRY #2

I finally got something published in The Review *and my roommate spread the only copy on the floor for the dog to pee on*

CR

JOURNAL ENTRY #3

There's never been too much communication between my parents and me, so when I was finally telling Dad what was important for me, I had to be careful I didn't shock him too much. But in a way there was a certain deception there because I had to tone down a lot of my views. What really struck me was the fact my dad wanted that deception there rather than what would have been the truth. It was like he had handed me a coloring book. As long as I used the right crayons and colored inside the lines, he would give a nod of approval.

BSJ

TGIF

Up until the day we killed Engfish, I had always considered students unappreciative and crass for roaring out of the campus so fast on Fridays, headed for home or the beach. I thought they should stay there and enjoy the rich cultural life the institution made available to them. And there were always their challenging studies, and a chance to utilize the wide and deep range of books in the university library so far superior to the one in their home town. Cutting out was childish, going back to Mommy and Daddy. Partying it up every weekend was crude.

Then one of my colleagues wrote a letter to the student newspaper pointing out what I had never sensed. The students wanted to get away from the dull, impersonal, pressured life of gigantic dorms and gigantic classes. They were so tamped down both inside and outside class from Monday through Friday, that they needed to explode.

That was what that noise was all about as cars burned rubber and varoomed away from the campus on Friday.

"Whereas it may fairly be said that
the personal equation
once in the days of scholastic learning
—was the central and decisive
factor in the systematization of knowledge,
it is equally fair to say
that in later time no effort is spared
to eliminate all bias of personality
from the technique or the results
of science or scholarship."

Thorstein Veblen,
The Higher Learning in America

Graduate School

PUBLIC WRITING

Several years ago, talking to an audience of college teachers at a national conference in Louisville, Kentucky, I read the following story by Louise Freyburger, one of John Bennett's students.

Reed

Maybe I could faint again. I did at the Solo-Ensemble Festival. Almost, anyway. That's where instrumentalists memorize a solo and go play it for a rating from some judge who knows all about whatever instrument it is and spends all his Saturdays listening to the same solos over and over. But I was playing along on mine and hoping I'd remember the next note because I'd only memorized the piece the night before and I kept getting short of breath and gulping. Pretty soon I felt faint, but I thought I better keep going instead of being one of those whimpering fainting females. I began wondering what would happen if I did faint right there.

It would wreck the reed for sure. The reed is what makes the noise. No reed, no sound, and the hellmost torture for a clarinetist is wrecking a reed because the good ones cost forty-five cents apiece and only come in boxes of ten and only two or three of these will work with luck, and two or three won't work at all, and the rest will just kind of thud a lot.

So when I thought of falling over on my good reed, I decided I better stop, so I asked the judge if I could stop for a while, except I said, "Sir, I feel faint." The judge was a heavy man who looked like he should have been bald, but he wasn't. Anyway, my accompanist hadn't heard me and it was at the end of a rest and I was supposed to come in again, so she kept playing my cue over and over. I walked over to the judge's desk and said I felt faint and wanted to sit down. He wore black glasses and looked at me over them like what was I doing stopping in the middle of a piece like that? I was supposed to just play and not interrupt his judging routine with sudden stops.

He took my elbow and my clarinet, which he put on his desk after checking the make of instrument and mouthpiece I had because he was a devoted clarinetist and probably hated fainting, whimpering females. I hoped then that I was using a fifteen-dollar Kaspar mouthpiece some character sits around making by hand in Ann Arbor, except he's retired now. This is like my mother telling me always to wear pretty underwear in case I get hit by a car and have to go to the hospital. Maybe she said that because once she fell down the stairs and broke her leg and was embarrassed to tears at having to ride all the way to the hospital in an ambulance with ugly underwear.

The judge kept my elbow and showed me to a chair. He told me to "take a whole bunch of deep breaths." While I was doing that, a group of people came into the room because they thought I was through playing. It was supposed to be a science classroom regularly except that Saturday when clarinetists performed in it and people were only allowed to come in between performances. When I got up and started in the middle of the solo, it puzzled them a little; but when I was through, they clapped anyway and the judge told them they hadn't heard very much, but the rest was just as good. That's one of those devious, double-sided comments people say and leave a person wondering exactly what they meant for some time afterward. I volunteered to play the whole thing again, but the judge kind of shoved me out to the hall and collapsed in a chair.

When I read that story aloud, a large part of the audience giggled and chuckled. John Ashmead, a novelist and teacher I know, was there, and I watched his face as I read because the paper delighted him.

But one teacher spoke up and said, "That is a charming bit of writing, but it's too personal. We need to teach our students *public* writing, which they must employ throughout college and in graduate school."

Graduate School

That woman in Louisville took me back to graduate school. I had started at the University of Wisconsin for a Ph.D., but the man I wanted to study under suddenly moved to Teachers College, Columbia. I felt I had to follow him to New York, but I didn't want to suffer through a whole raft of Education courses. I arranged a Ph.D. at Columbia, but had to take most of my work at Teachers College.

There I studied the new Linguistics under a disciple of C. C. Fries, a pioneer in language study. I learned that linguists agree that the average child masters the major elements of the grammar of his language by the age of five or six. He may say, "I gots a gun," or "Me and Johnny played in the tree," but those deviations from standard patterns are proportionately rare. In that class I saw how complex American-English grammar is—requiring an intelligent selection from thousands of options of word order, or meaning does not arise in a sentence. Later when I began to observe children on my own, I found sure enough they had mastered those subtleties in ninety per cent of their utterance. They never said, "Have Mom can Popsicle a I?" They never said, "What are we going to have of dinner?" They knew idiom and commanded word order, the principal grammatical signal of their language. And they had learned those intricacies in three or four years *without going to school.*

With that awareness, the linguists and I should have asked, "Why then teach grammar to them from first grade into college?" But we didn't. Our reverend forefathers accurately used the term "grammar schools." What went on there then and goes on there today is as insane and demoralizing as if year after year in every grade a child were taught the fundamentals of walking just because he occasionally drags a heel or scuffs his toes. "Now we will have parts of the leg: thigh, lower leg, foot. In walking, the foot should always be kept at the bottom of the leg."

THE HAM TEST

Looking back to my graduate school days, I realize where the notion that American students are dull and inept human beings comes from. At the highest reaches of teaching, where adults are studying for the Ph.D. and M.A. degrees, students are demeaned, and there they learn the arts of demeaning others.

Every six months or so the head of my department in that graduate school would hold receptions at his apartment and I would tell my wife I wouldn't go, but I always went. There one evening I remember one of my fellow students was asked to slice the ham. I think it was the head's wife who asked him, ever so gaily, so that everyone could hear. He trembled, a young man with few social graces and reason to believe he was on the edge of flunking out of graduate school. He said he'd rather not, and was led to the table and given the knife. One of my friends leaned over to me and whispered that this was the symbolic carving. Each year, he said, a questionable man is treated in this manner. Mr. F wanted more than academic respectability from a prospective teacher: he wanted self-discipline and command. If the student were truly to represent Teachers College and this department, wouldn't he eventually rise to a position of eminence, as Professor F had, perhaps the presidency of the National Council of Teachers of English or the Conference on College Composition and Communication? I felt the knife going through the young man who was holding it. He turned red like the ham. He sweated, he did not carve neat slices. I don't know now for sure whether he ever got his degree, but I think not.

PUBLIC OPINION

What did that woman in Louisville mean by *public* writing? I thought of a professor from whom I took a course in Public Opinion at Columbia University proper, across the street from Teachers College. He was pure graduate school, leaned his head over his notes every day, mumbled into them, never looked up to see what we were doing out there—not more than twelve students at most—except to say angrily a couple of times that he knew many of us did not read completely the three books assigned. He told us what he thought of those works and the men who had written them. He laughed at his jokes, which few of us found funny, and I began to cut class. I had already read the third book, *Public Opinion* by Walter Lippmann, because it touched upon my thesis subject. It has affected my thinking ever since. But despite, or maybe because of, the professor's praise for James Bryce's *The American Commonwealth,* I read only a few pages in it. The old man—I say that as a considered description; for he seemed tired of talking to classes, physically and mentally—talked a lot about himself, as he had a right to do, being the chief counter among sociologists in the whole country.

But his talk was seldom entertaining or instructive. I saw no great mind at play and therefore doubted that its work had been what it was claimed to be. Like so many, he seemed not to live the life he advocated, or anything like it. He was talking all those hours and days about public opinion. Unlike Walter Lippmann, he seemed not very interested in people. He had a small public in front of him. He never got to know them. The implication was that they were not worth knowing and surely could not say anything that would be news to a Great Man.

SEMINAR

"Public writing," the woman said. I remembered a seminar I took at Teachers College. There, I thought, we would be writing for the other mature students around the table, a public, and our writing would take on a liveness and dignity that it could not possess when students wrote only for Teacher.

I felt beside myself with luck, for I had the chance to take this seminar taught by the head of the department, Mr. F, who was a pioneer in borrowing from other fields to shake up the teaching of English, and Mr. E, famous for bringing the deep and unadulterated world of great books to the public on network commercial radio. Now in the big city the study of English would be for real.

The first day was true T.C. The two men excited us as they suggested the possibilities of the course. We could learn from everything, and the man from the network downtown would give us a sense of the agonies of communicating with real publics, a sense Professor F wisely admitted he was not likely to furnish.

The second meeting of the seminar gave us what were to be the realities of the course. Neither teacher knew what he wanted to say. I expected that from Professor F, who was always sketching in the air more than talking to a class, but not from Mr. E, who as a professional radio broadcaster surely knew he must have a script in hand or mind when he went on the air. After two meetings of embarrassing undirected talking at us, the two began the practice of retiring from the room for a few minutes when Mr. E arrived ten or twenty minutes late from his pressing and impressive duties downtown. They would return confident and smiling. They had planned the afternoon's seminar.

These two professors thought they knew so much more than we students that they could talk off the cuff and make each minute valuable. Such an attitude prevents a man from seeing what in his experience will be new and stimulating to others. They failed to bring their best to that seminar because they didn't believe we were worth it.

Death by Degrees

But the most famous teachers' college in the country couldn't advocate demeaning students, so it talked a lot about respecting them. I was named president of a little club founded by the head of the department. It was a front. We graduate students did what the professors wanted us to do to make the department look good.

One of the members of the organization told me he was being forced to do something in his thesis he didn't believe in, and asked the club to discuss the matter with the head of the department—as a matter of policy. We called a meeting of our tiny group and decided we should speak in the student's behalf. I told a professor what we were going to do. He was shocked. To think we would dare suggest to the head of the department what he should do in regard to advising a student on writing the sacred document. He said softly, "I don't think it would be wise." We followed his suggestion. We wanted our degrees. We were prepared to die for them, I think.

Fulfilling a Vow

When I was head of that little association of graduate students, that Establishment front, I spent a goodly amount of time in the hallways listening to tales of neglect and sadism from my fellow students. I understood their impulse: they had to tell someone about the wrongs they felt they were suffering, but they should have known that none of us students would jeopardize his professional career by exposing the professors. I vowed that someday when I was free, I would publish the story to the world.

Approximately ten years later, as editor of *College Composition and Communication*, a journal of the National Council of Teachers of English, I asked ten persons I knew to write case-histories of their experience as graduate students. They were working for or had just obtained degrees from large universities in the North, South, East, and West. I chose them because they could write, and I let them say what they wanted to. Of the ten histories I printed (in the December, 1964 issue) only one reported a positive experience. Here are excerpts from each of the ten:

1. *I could not recommend the total experience to anyone.*
2. *Literature here is studied as if it were a dead cat. . .*
3. *This graduate school is no treadmill. . .*
4. *Consider the program as a package.*
5. *One wins a Ph.D. by being a drudge.*
6. *The graduate school obstructed the exchange of ideas.*
7. *. . . an interruption rather than a preparation. . .*
8. *I was regarded as an adolescent.*
9. *I was thrown a bunch of A's and B's to eat.*
10. *A nagging sense of dislocation. . .*

Grad School Has Not Changed

Today I received a letter from a former student now in graduate school. I am saddened to find her experience no different from mine twenty years ago. She is attending the most reputable university in the midwest.

Dear Dr. Macrorie,

I expect to finish my Master's degree this month and am planning to find a job for next fall teaching English at a junior college or small university. So I'm filling out placement papers and would like your recommendation as part of my file.

I haven't been very satisfied with school here, neither with the University nor with myself. The faculty advisor for my half of the alphabet is a busy man whose greatest concern is getting people out of his office and out of the Master's program as soon as possible. And two five-minute sessions with him have been my sole contact with the administration, so I am left feeling that the Master's degree is a necessary evil in the eyes of the English Department.

And then the classes seem oriented toward preparing us to pass the qualifying exams for doctoral study. This is particularly true of my B—— lit class, where the professor is basing our grades for the course entirely on the final exam—which he is preparing and grading as if it were the B—— section on the qualifying exam. Now it's only practical that a person who's going on for a Ph.D. should worry about passing the qualifiers; but when the professor acknowledges that as the purpose of study, I begin to wish for less practicality and more interest in English literature.

Class size is relatively large (30-35 people, except for a proseminar of about 10), and usually the professor lectures, with more or less class discussion thrown in. I seldom say anything in class and I'm not sure why. Mostly because I lack confidence and there are so many other people who don't. So they do the talking or the professor does. I don't like that because I'm interested in what's going on and it makes me feel stupid that I don't contribute, though I do well on papers and exams and have an A- average. But I'm not really involved in my classes, and beyond some guilt feelings, I'm not motivated to get involved.

Writing papers is a chore that leaves me uninterested in what I've written, even though I started with an original good idea. And a Master's degree seems to be a super-grade that's only necessary for going on to the next step.

Maybe I'm just tired of school. At any rate, my classes are happening on the edges of my life, and I hope the fault is not all mine. I'd like a more leisurely, creative (utopian) graduate school with tiny classes and no worries about future exams. Until I find some place closer to that ideal than this university I don't feel like going on for a doctorate—or until I get over my present restlessness I want to teach now because I need something I can really put myself into and feel that I'm being useful, that I'm doing a respectable, worthwhile job.

Mark Van Doren

In recalling my graduate school days at Columbia University, I remembered Mark Van Doren, who seemed a god. He never talked of horizons or perspectives in T.C. style, but of what Huck Finn or he as a boy had seen when they emerged from a cave.

Like every good man, Mr. Van Doren had never grown up. He walked into class and onto the high platform smiling as if he had been caught doing something slightly naughty, and then told us what he had seen that day which connected him to Don Quixote or Hamlet at the graveside. On the papers we wrote for that course in the nature of tragedy and comedy, he never marked our errors. I remember a little vertical line in the margin and the word "good" next to it. A little further down, "better." I treasured that second word because I knew Mr. Van Doren meant it and he knew what he was talking about.

When I asked to talk about one of my papers, he chatted directly and amiably and pointed to a place where I had apologized for disagreeing with such an eminent authority as Joseph Wood Krutch. Mr. Van Doren said, "You don't have to apologize. I'm sure Mr. Krutch would respect your argument."

In many books I have admired I have noticed in the front an acknowledgement to Mark Van Doren for encouraging the writer. I am sure that was his strength as a teacher.

During his lectures I often took down his humorous and pointed comments to read later to friends. He gave no tests. But the class of about forty students was dead. Seldom did he ask for a comment or question. Often only about sixty per cent of the class showed up. I was thrilled to listen to a man thinking before me, seriously, playfully; and yet he had come prepared. But I don't think I learned much, because I was never invited to commit myself, and neither was any other student. Mark Van Doren could have changed the lives of every student in that room had he known how to awaken and encourage those students in the classroom as he did the writers who sat in his office talking of their work, or who received letters of criticism from him after they had graduated.

But Mark Van Doren never demeaned his students

"The educational program is designed
to give the student
a foundation in each of the great
areas of knowledge."

—from a college catalog

Undergraduate Days

Undergraduate Guilt

Thinking of graduate school led me all the way back to my undergraduate days at Oberlin College in Ohio. In the first three years there the central feeling I experienced was guilt. My mother, a widow, was working hard back in Illinois to put me through college. I had been given a two-year tuition scholarship which required a B average. In freshman and sophomore years my grades hovered between C+ and B. I was allowed to keep the scholarship, but each semester I thought I would lose it.

Oberlin College impressed me—one couldn't find a higher academic reputation—but I found myself wanting to take off for Cleveland every weekend to hear Louis Armstrong or Count Basie instead of staying on campus and studying. I tried to study but couldn't keep my mind on the work. Never occurred to me that both my professors and I were doing C+ work.

Intellectual

In my sophomore year, 1937-38, I signed up for the wrong courses. One was *The Intellectual History of Western Europe from St. Augustine to Karl Marx,* in which we read twenty or so masterpieces. As usual, I remembered the names of every one, and today I can tell you that Thomas à Kempis wrote *The Imitation of Christ* and how to spell *Aucassin and Nicolette,* but I haven't the smallest idea of what was in the books. The first one was religious and the second a love story—I can't say more. In those days the remarkable fact to me was that a day after I had read a book I couldn't remember enough to answer questions on three of the ten points the professor touched upon in lectures.

That course was a crime, taught by one of the most famous of Oberlin professors at the time. A little man, Professor K came to class every day laden with books he slapped down on the desk, which stood high above the seats on a platform. He smacked his lips and told jokes I didn't understand and showed off until I thought he must be standing there in his underwear.

One day he was lecturing furiously at five minutes into the hour when in walked a graduate student I knew, an older fellow who had just returned from a year's study abroad. He walked unobtrusively to his seat in the front—under the professor's gaze, mounted as he was upon his pedestal—and sat down. I don't remember what Mr. K was saying, but he was moving along, a train clacketing on the rails, and without change of pitch or speed he finished a sentence and said, "and anyone who thinks he can come into this class five minutes late and interrupt the lecture, had just better not come at all."

Because the hour had hardly begun, my attention was still working, and I heard every word. At the instant the professor finished that remark, the student arose, hurried to the door in the left corner of the room behind the professor, opened it, went through it, and slammed it with a bang that shook the old frame of Peters Hall. Professor K was stunned into several seconds of silence. I wanted to stand and cheer. Swallowing hard, K continued the lecture, but the fire was gone from his voice. I believe this is the only instance I have observed in all my college years as a student of one of the slaves successfully reversing his role of the demeaned.

BONGIORNO

Undergraduate classes were not all lectures, and two were genuine seminars of the kind Teachers College promised but never delivered. In one, Andrew Bongiorno sat straight in his chair at the end of the big table, seldom showing his feeling about our comments on each other's papers and never revealing which of us he thought had been the ablest persuader. He graded the papers, but there he had little to say, because most of it had already been said by us students.

We learned fast how to make each other face our assertions for what they were and where they had carried us. We didn't cover Aristotle's *Poetics* or *Rhetoric* that year, only took up a few central principles and applied them rigorously to plays that were worth examining.

We did not learn to be purists. One night after the reading of a paper, the oldest student in the class said in ministerial tones, "I know this is a small matter, but we are all English majors and I think we must never allow ourselves the kind of sloppiness in diction just evidenced. The reader of the last paper said a certain action was the *most perfect* instance of something. Now a thing can be perfect, but it cannot be *more perfect* or *most perfect*." He sat back in his chair pleased, and then three of us laid into him, saying he was a purist fool and that we could quote a number of fine writers who said *most perfect*, and one of my friends came up with an example on the spot.

Mr. Bongiorno sat there saying nothing. A quick smile of amusement passed over his face. He was not lecturing in that class, but he saw his students constantly learning.

A student in Room 241 Eng T took up the first fifteen minutes having the instructor explain what he said the day before—then fell asleep.

DESPAIR

A WARM GUN

I am thinking of a meeting at my university several years ago, a symposium on *Change in the University,* sponsored by the Honors College, encouraged by the president and academic dean of the university. It was widely announced weeks ahead of time. Four meetings were planned: with faculty, student, and administration speakers, and finally, a brave and brilliant United States Senator. None of the meetings was well attended; I suppose the university community felt that anything said under official auspices on such an explosive issue in a year of campus demonstrations and protests and violence would be hogwash.

The meetings were not rigged. The three student speakers invited were a past president of the Student Association, a liberal; the current president of the Student Association, who had joined SDS after gaining the presidency; and one of the editors of *The Activist,* a student underground paper that had been slashing away at the administration for several years.

When the students began speaking, there were about thirty-five people in the audience. I counted five professors who had come to hear what students had to say about campus revolution.

During the question and answer period, a black student walked down the aisle and spoke to the two radical students, whom he apparently knew.

"*This is all very nice, what you said, that the university is a bad place and all that, but what do you expect me to do about it? What can I do right now? You answer me that.*"

"*Well,*" said the president of the Student Association, "*I'm asking you when you see something wrong, to expose it for what it is. Write about it in* The Activist, *for example.*"

"*No, you don't get me. I'm asking about doing, not writing. You think I can really change anything around here? Or you just talking? There's sixty students in my class. What do you expect me to do?*"

The president, former SDSer, was disconcerted. He took the question seriously. "*It all depends on how much you're willing to risk. You can raise your hand, stand up, and say you don't like the reading assignments and think they should be changed.*"

"*Yeah,*" said the questioner, smiling, "*I could do that.*"

"*You could—as I said—only if you're willing to risk some-*

thing. In this case, your position as student, and perhaps your life in Vietnam."

"That's right."

"You could speak only if you're willing to be shot down. Because the professor carries a revolver in his holster and it's loaded with grades. He doesn't like what you say, he points it at you and 'F,' you're out."

"That's right, man."

Aim

During that meeting on *Change in the University*, the *Activist* editor had nothing positive to say about the university or the country. At one point he condemned the mass media for presenting a completely distorted view of the radical student movement.

But the president of the Student Association, also an SDS member, suggested that if anyone in the audience did not understand what the SDS was up to nationally, he should read the article in the current *Look* magazine, which he said showed accurately how democratically the organization was run. I found the contradiction between these two radicals' comments on the mass media not surprising. One of the central aims of the university is to build the habit of looking at facts before coming to a judgment, but this is only an aim in the catalog. In the classroom the aim is more likely to be that of a gun, as the little colloquy at the symposium brought out.

THE INSTITUTION WON'T EVER CHANGE ITSELF

On the day they left for California in an old Volkswagen bus, four college dropouts visited me in my office. We talked two hours.

Jim: *I've come more and more to believe you should do what you've got to do right now, whatever it is.*

Brad: *Yeah. All this planning ahead ruins everything. Parents or bankers are always saying, "You must think of the consequences of your acts right now." Well I say bullshit. You can ruin a lot of things that way.*

Jim: *But on the other hand, to get something projected, something fairly big that's got to be accomplished with other people you have to think about it a little ahead of time. And then you're in the bag of organization, and everything's ruined. Because you can't work with the other people.*

Brad: *That's why I don't trust the new revolutionary leaders, either. Pretty soon they are bossing everyone around.*

Professor: But what about the black students holding the Student Union for a day? Didn't the Administration back down and for a change do what you wanted them to do?

Sally: *No. For a few minutes the Administration held back its power, like a bubble in the airflow, but only so there wouldn't be too much commotion, and then the next day everything would be back to normal again. And that's the way it was. They didn't give up any power permanently.*

Jim: *The way I feel these days, I don't think there's any hope for this country. Reason won't win out. The Establishment will just continue to exercise its power. It will give in a little when it has to, but it will come right back strong.*

Sally: *Right. That's why there's got to be more than what you say you're trying—a reform from within. The institution won't ever change itself. It's got to be confronted in some massive way. And I've gotten to feel now that I don't care what happens to this country. It's not worth saving.*

Brad: *Me neither. It sounds terrible, but it's true. I don't give a damn whether the university is burned down or the country goes smash. I couldn't care less. What would be lost?*

GOODBYE TO ALL THAT

I asked Bob Koehler, a young man who had been editor of *The Western Review*, a paper that published a good deal of writing from Third Way classes, to give me a picture of the classroom that revealed his feelings about the university. He handed me this statement after he had dropped out of school.

I have lots of random stories about injustices and hurt feelings caused by the pompous indifference of people involved in my formal education experience, but can no longer find the passion to try to retell any, no more than I'd be interested in portraying the unfairness of the spanking Mommy gave me for peeing on the floor when really it was just my sister spilled some water and was afraid to tell the truth. I have been away from the niggling squabbles and demands of this darkling campus for so long I am beyond bitterness, and let those three armies called faculty, administration, and student body clash their bloody heads together all they want. Just let me alone; I'm into my own things. I know I can learn more by myself, with the help of my friends. Not only beyond bitterness, beyond hope and sympathy for this place. The university has invented too many problems for itself.

If a professor really wants to reach his students, give them the feel of Chaucer or Marx, have them grasp concepts that have changed his life, he's going to have to question all the facets of the university and consider the fact that a kid can maybe learn more in a concentrated weekend seminar or a casual conversation free from distractions like wretched dorm life and the inane pressures of The Grade, and uncomfortable poorly designed classrooms, and oops! the hour is up again, try not to forget it all by Monday—else, professor, you're just playing Parcheesi, the students are the pieces and you try to move them from here to there (if indeed you're playing the game seriously) on the arbitrary board-of-education provided by our society. I'm out of that game.

Drop out and return

Malcolm Huey left the university to find a Free School in California. He found one and now is back in Michigan again enrolled at the University, as is Bob Koehler, who tried to make himself and the immediate environment his own school.

Something apparently was missing in the freedom they found, as something is missing in the traditional university. In the former, I suspect it is regularity, responsibility, security. In the latter, freedom to use one's personal, authentic powers.

For both young men the return to the established institution will be agonizing. After their disillusionment with the way of absolute freedom, they may be more charitable toward the university for a while; but I think it will finally dry up their vital juices with its registration lines, tests, questions, reading lists, assignments.

And in their middle twenties.

POWERLESS

Bob Koehler, Malcolm Huey, and other intelligent university students I know are probably powerless to change the university into a moving place for learning. They can force the college president or the trustees to moderate the rules for dormitory living or institute courses in black studies, but when they attack the professor in his citadel, the classroom, they will find out what power means. Under the sweet-sounding name of *academic freedom* the professor has built in all kinds of protections from outside criticism.

When the challenge comes, the administrator, who is constantly attacked by most professors for being too conservative about everything on campus, will side with the professor. For example:

> . . . this University stands for freedom of speech, freedom of inquiry, freedom of dissent and freedom to demonstrate in a peaceful manner. In taking this stand, the University points out that there cannot be freedom without some measure of order. .
>
> If any attempt is made by an individual or group to disrupt your classes there are three steps that should be taken in line with [the president's] statement:
>
> 1. The disruptors should be directed to leave.
> 2. If they do not, you or someone you designate should immediate call Safety and Security (3-1880) or the University Switchboard (3-1600) with the request that the disruption be reported to the security staff, and assistance be requested. Be sure to give the number of the room as well as the building to which they are to report.
> 3. Every effort should be made to identify the persons involved by obtaining information from eye witnesses or in any other proper manner. The names of such persons, and the names of eye witnesses to the disruption should then be forwarded to the Dean of Students in a written report so that alleged participants in disruptive activities may be subject to appropriate disciplinary action under established procedures.

What is disruption?

Obviously, a student who rises in a class to assert that the assignment is dead, the test a waste of time, or the lecture an impediment to student discussion is disrupting the course.

Call in the police before any free exchange of ideas occurs.

Needed

I fear that the movement of students to reform university teaching, if carried out by them alone, will end in a wave of breaking windows and burning offices. In that struggle the students do not have enough power. They can quit school and put the professor out of a job, but what they need is a reformed pro fessor working hard at his job.

One of the free schools recently
established in Vancouver,
British Columbia,
is called Knowplace.

Hope

HOPE

Yet I have a great deal of hope for universities. In this country and in Britain and Canada, there are individuals stirring who see educational power as something different from economic or military power.

In the Third Way the professor and student do not contest for power to keep each other down. When the student is moving upwards, using all his abilities and extending and sharpening them, the professor is at his most powerful. When he quits using instruments of boredom and torture, he finds his students doing and saying things that make him look good.

The realist's common response to suggestion of reform from within—"You expect the men with power to give it up for someone else's good?"—is based on a misconception. The professors teaching with traditional methods do not have a satisfying power now, except as sadism is satisfying to a few. Most often, professors feel bored and defeated. Their students are not learning what they want them to learn.

So both professors and students stand to gain from reform which takes the Third Way.

THE REFORM HAS BEGUN

Already the New Math has been blessed in the universities and applied in the schools. Much of the rote instruction of arithmentic and algebra has been replaced by teaching which anticipates that the student on his own will be able to see relationships that speak to each other and to him as well. No longer simply, "Memorize this formula."

An astounding change in teaching.

Already foreign languages are being taught to ears instead of eyes so that tongues can communicate with sounds.

An astounding change in teaching.

BEGINNINGS

Already in England the Cambridge University Press in the last five years has published a number of books by David Holbrook which condemn the little tortures devised by composition teachers in Britain. He asserts and demonstrates that almost every child in the schools has not only had unique and significant experiences which command our respect, but can often communicate them vigorously if encouraged to do so.

In the United States the number of formidable men who teach and write about teaching a New English grows. Jerome Bruner has long recognized the likeness between the scientist who works at the leading edge of his field and the writer who constructs a precise and liberating metaphor. Mr. Bruner sees the schoolboy and university student capable of paralleling the processes of the scientist and writer.

Benjamin De Mott, a novelist and critic at Amherst, has recently begun to teach himself and other teachers across the country how to open up students to a full use of their already acquired resources. As both an artist and a free-lance writer of articles for mass media, Mr. DeMott reaches professors with an experience and eloquence that they envy.

At Massachusetts Institute of Technology, Peter Elbow has begun to write about the teaching of English with an insight and grace that led the editor of the journal *College English* to give him more space than I think any other author has been accorded in the history of this respected publication. Sample of Mr. Elbow's writing:

> I warn against defining sincerity as telling true things about oneself. It is more accurate to define it functionally as the sound of the writer's voice or self on paper—a general sound of authenticity in the words. The point is that self revelation—breast baring (going topless)—is an easy route in our culture and therefore can be used as an evasion: it can be functionally insincere even if substantively true and intimate. To be precise, ***sincerity is the absence of "noise" or static—the ability or courage not to hide the real message.***

WORD FROM BELOW

John Holt in *How Children Fail* and *How Children Learn*, Herbert Kohl in *36 Children*, and James Herndon in *The Way It Spozed to Be* have convinced a number of university teachers that children in elementary school and junior high school have something valid to say on paper. Soon the professors—large numbers of them—will be ready to admit the same is true for their students.

Over a year ago *Life* magazine ran an article by Judson Jerome, a poet who teaches at Antioch College, telling how he conducts classes that respect students as resourceful human beings. These days every time I attend a teachers' conference or consult with teachers or students anywhere in the nation, I run into persons who practice all or some of the methods of the Third Way. And not only in publicly supported institutions. Recently I have worked with teachers at a Jesuit university and a Seventh Day Adventist university who were anxious to hear of ways to break students loose from the goose-step of traditional education.

A number of the college graduates who are today going into teaching know the Establishment schools have done badly by them. They are ready to try new ways, and many have the courage to try them even at the risk of losing their jobs.

COURSE PRESCRIPTION

For years I asked to teach a course in the Criticism of Mass Media. When I got the chance, both at San Francisco State and Western Michigan University, my students did badly. They did not even show the vague feelings of friendliness and appreciation that my teaching always used to engender.

A colleague and I wrote the course description for the catalog:

> A study of the nature of the mass media and a development of standards for criticizing them.

We were proud of the statement. It did not seem academically polluted.

After I found the Third Way, I realized that the course description by omission conveyed the usual implication—the students would not be expected to engage in criticism and to sharpen themselves at the task until what they said or wrote was valuable to them and to others. Rather they would read what the experts had said and "develop" (read: "memorize for the test") what the teacher and his fellow critics thought were proper standards.

The Patient in a Critical Stage

Each year I struggle with the Mass Media class. I try to show the students through their own journal comments on films and TV shows and magazine ads that they already know a great deal about mass communications and often can read pictures better than I can.

But when I invite them to comment, they sit there in the U of seats in the small classroom, about 25 of them, and look at each other, as if trying to avoid my gaze and the chance of being called upon, although they know I will never question them individually. Or they look down at their feet. Damn you, I think. Say something!

I asked them one day to take home a weekday copy of *The New York Times* and study it as the great naturalist Louis Agassiz asked his Harvard graduate students to study a fish on a lab tray. An hour. Tell me what you saw. Four hours. Tell me what you saw. Forty hours. You are beginning to get a sense of the fish.

I knew my students weren't looking at the *Times*. They weren't developing a capacity for independent observation or for generalizing rigorously on close examination of details.

And when I think of their indoctrination, why should they? I ask them to look at a film or newspaper and put down what they see. "What does he wan.?" they are constantly saying as they look, seeing nothing for themselves.

SELF-HEAL IS A BEAUTIFUL BLUE

This year when the journals came in to me in the Mass Media class I was almost destroyed by the small number of entries most students had made. And the naiveté of many of the comments.

Only a half dozen students had acted upon invitation (not an assignment) to see the black militant Le Roi Jones's short film *Dutchman*, which was playing three times in one day free on campus. Why should they go? I told them I would not grade any of their work until mid-semester; other courses, with their tests and term papers, all to be graded, pressed harder upon them.

I opened a student journal to an entry on the film:

I have mixed feelings about Dutchman, *but all in all, I feel it was certainly the worst movie I have ever seen. I didn't quite know how to take it. It was repulsive. It's bad enough that things like this go on in the world, but do we have to make movies about them? There's enough rubbish in the world . . . .*

What could I do with a girl who wrote like that after six weeks in my course? I began phrasing in my mind scathing remarks to wake that class up. I read on.

The movie left me quite confused, with many questions. What did the movie really signify? I think it was race—again, black versus white. The black man played along with the white woman to a point and then he pulled himself together and turned on her, realizing this was all wrong. He didn't want to be a part of this sick white woman's scene after all, whatever it was. Does this somehow reflect society today? The title also left me unsure. The dictionary defines being "in dutch" as being in trouble or disgraced, and this is, I believe, what the title had in mind. The black man ended up being disgraced by the white woman. He himself didn't feel right about it.

What about the apples and the one orange that the woman peeled? Why did she take a bite of the apple and then toss it out? or toss out what she had just bit out of it? Perhaps the apple goes back to Adam and Eve in the Garden of Eden. We have the other people in the subway. Was that our society just sitting there so apathetically? They just sat quietly by while the black man was stabbed to death by the white woman. Then what really got me was when she was back to do the whole thing over again. Was this a hack on our justice or sometimes the lack of it? The entire movie seemed very unreal to me. What good was it? I couldn't find any value in it. It certainly wasn't a fun movie or something you would go to for enjoyment. Maybe it's an awakening for some people. I have all the questions, but none of the answers.

I was angry reading that entry. It would take twenty years for me to get this girl thinking instead of just automatically reacting, I thought, automatically reacting myself. I read on in her journal and found another entry, on *The New York Times,* which clicked something in my head. I remembered a paper I had just received in Shakespeare class in which a bright student had said:

> Richard II *bothers me as a play. I find it shallow and totally confusing. I see Richard in the same perspective.*

This student wrote almost the identical words the girl had written about *Dutchman.* He said, "*The whole play is full of questions with no real answers.*" Then like her, he began to speculate on answers, and wisely. Both students were giving the other students and me an honest record of their reactions to a work of art: the initial confusion, the uncomfortableness with new modes and surprising materials, and then the attempt to find order and meaning in the work changing so rapidly before them.

I had to hang on, to give those Mass Media students many chances to fail or stumble or refuse to try the steps. I began to see that although the girl who had written about *Dutchman* had begun and ended with what is often called a "WASP (White Anglo Saxon Protestant) reaction"—a condemning and pushing away of anything that questions or breaks up traditional patterns of thought and feeling—that within this frame of thoughtlessness, she had recorded a number of lines that probed and often came up with good guesses about what this artist, so far from her in experience, had been trying to do in his film.

OTHER WEEDS WITH BENEFICENT INFLUENCE

Right within that journal entry the girl who wrote about *Dutchman* was making her move, from an angry declaration of her right to refuse to open herself to new and alien and frightening experience, to beginning this very opening. In the next journal I opened, I found an entry on *Dutchman* which when read in class would move the first writer further.

An explosive movie is the only way to describe Dutchman, *the story of a young middle-class Negro male who was propositioned by a shapely white prostitute on a New York subway. Seems at first to be an example of perverted entertainment, but slowly changes tone and turns into a racial conflict in principle. The writer tries to present misconceptions and stereotypes of blacks held by whites and vice versa. The conservative black man who was white and middle class in everything except his culture at the end of the show rightfully stood up for his culture after a lot of harassing and with rather a symbolic meaning was rewarded for his outburst by a knife blade in his chest from his white companion.*

The movie has an unreal dream-like quality in its absence of people in the subway, which helps the viewer focus more on the underlying meaning of the story. . .

BREAKING OUT

And then I read this third entry about *Dutchman* in a journal.

Are these real people? Is the director trying to put a particular message across? The Dutchman is a long train ride. A developing relationship between a black man and a white woman. At the hands of the woman tragedy and death befall the black man and a feeling of unconcern is felt by everyone but the audience. A person might say, "Of course, the film is giving a message, can't you see? It's showing the inner feelings of the black man, and all the ridicule, sarcasm, and mockery he has had to endure." Yes, I can sense this feeling; but I ask again, "Are these real people?" Is the film giving equal representation to both sides? We have a normal upper middle class black business man. Fine, what else do we have? We have a sick, sick woman who is striking out against the black society when she herself would not be accepted by her own. One might say, "Well, this film shows the overall view of the situation." But I have yet to find one person who will identify with the girl on the train. I cannot associate this picture with anything in my reality. This is a picture with a message. It radiates feeling, and you find yourself cheering for the good guy. The good guy is black. But that makes little difference. You would cheer him if he was red, purple, or pink. The film is well done, and many different opinions will develop from it. This is mine.

The honesty of this response gives it validity and perhaps gives validity to what I think is LeRoi Jones's point—the white man cannot associate himself with this reality, this systematic demeaning of another human being. But beyond that fundamental point, this entry touches many of the crucial questions about contemporary art and society. Does the film put together realistic and unrealistic elements? If so, do they work together even though they defy the ancient dramatic unities? What is the relation of the dream world in this film to the real world? Can a film-maker or writer mesh the two successfully in one work?

In discussing *Dutchman* another student quoted lines from Ralph Ellison's *Invisible Man*. They described precisely the ambience in which the characters move in *Dutchman*. And they threw light upon the film for the whole class.

Many of the journals I looked through in that class at the halfway point in the semester seemed almost primitive in their observations. Now I realize that that is the way they should seem, coming from students who have been deprived of minds and tongues in schoolrooms for twelve years or more. I must encourage and wait, watching for the signs of walking upright or the first intelligent use of the opposable thumb.

News from New Schools

Two years ago a friend sent me a subscription to *This Magazine Is About Schools,* a quarterly published in Toronto (P.O. Box 876, Terminal A) by a group of young persons who report what New Schools and Free Schools are doing today. In photographs, reproductions of Free School students' work, reports of what young people are thinking and doing inside and outside conventional schools. *This Magazine* is stunning. I have seen nothing like it in all my years of examining magazines as a student of mass communication.

Sample from Peter Marin's article "Adolescence and the Apocalypse":

> Early in the school year we had found ourselves going to great lengths to provide vivid experiences *within* the school: encounter groups, psychodrama, team-teaching, independent study, curricular changes, less traditional content—all of the innovational devices of contemporary pedagogy. Some worked better than others but none worked as well, in general, as direct social experience. The simple fact seemed to be that our students grew when they were allowed to move freely into and around the adult community; when they were not, they languished. (Spring, 1969, p. 55)

Freedom to follow the direction of one's own movement and the *Discipline* of considering the response of others to it.

The Third Way

PRINCIPLES AT WORK

Put the *here* principle to work in any university course. Political science, for instance.

What is the student's experience in political science? He has read a few textbooks and gone on a phony field trip to the State Capitol, where the guide let him sit in his senator's chair, told him how high the ceilings were, and showed him the tattered flag carried at Gettysburg. He has not voted in a national election or a city election.

Six years ago, before I stumbled onto the Third Way, that would have been my assessment of my beginning student had I been teaching a political science course.

Now it would be different. I know that the student has probably participated in elections of the Student Council in high school. Or has refused to participate, out of cynicism. In the university the election of officers for the Student Association is coming up soon. The student probably knows or suspects the powerlessness of such a political arrangement. Probably student power in his institution has been growing under the prodding of activists. The system is intriguing because it is in a state of flux.

Or the student has attended dorm meetings or committees of some student organization where he observed how real and pseudo power contended with each other. Somewhere in campus life around him—or outside the campus in the workings of another hierarchy, perhaps church, labor, or fraternity—lies a *here* for the student to investigate. Once he begins that investigation, he has something to compare with the *theres* which the professor would like him to think about. Then is the time to pursue some truths, when student and professor share their expert knowledge and their experience.

FIRST AND FOREMOST

As they lecture to hundreds of students in an auditorium or administer a massive multiple-choice test to thousands in the fieldhouse, many professors do not realize that they are treating college students as children are treated in the most punitive elementary schools. At a higher level, with more sophistication, they carry out little acts every day which reveal them as no less tyrants than does this memo to parents, distributed by an elementary school my step-daughters attended three years ago:

For the Greenfield Trip Chaperones

> First and foremost is the matter of discipline. It is of the utmost importance that all be on their best behavior—no loud talking on the bus anywhere,—no running, pushing, or any other rude behavior,—no handling of objects not their own,—no littering anywhere. If it becomes necessary to use disciplinary action, do it immediately and later report it to the child's teacher. . . .
>
> The children in your group are to be within arm's reach at all times. NO RUNNING AHEAD. They are to find YOU and STAY with you.

[The professor in his classroom says, "I'd like you to do some reading on your own, as you suggest; but I must remind you I cannot give extra credit for it because all class work is graded, and every student must be judged on the same basis."]

> It will not be your job to find them. They are to ask permission to do anything that the group is not doing. There are many restrooms, and group trips to them should be made often. Punishment for disobedience for wandering off should be made.

[The professor says, "That's a good question, but I don't think we should entertain it now because it's off the point of our discussion."]

> It is not a contest to see which group can finish first. In order to see the displays properly, one must go slowly, read the signs, and listen to the lectures. This is not an outing. It is an educational experience. . .

In the Field

Not every university teacher feels that way about field trips. Some of them have made the trips honest-to-God journeys for the participants, not guided tours. Students of Italian art are sent to live in Italy for a year. Students of ghetto life work in the slums. At my university journalism and broadcasting students take an internship with a newspaper or television station. Small changes in universities have made them ready for big ones.

Kings

But a student does not have to travel in Great Britain to get with King Lear. In the Third Way students easily and naturally connect their class work with the world they know outside the classroom.

At 6:00 a.m. on the Friday after Martin Luther King, Jr., was assassinated, about two hundred black students at my university sneaked in the huge Student Union and chained shut all the doors. They held the building for eight hours, eating in its cafeteria in orderly fashion, paying for their meals, cleaning the building before they finally left. Outside, hundreds of white students gathered, some complaining they were being denied the use of their building, separated from morning coffee in the Snack Bar.

In my Shakespeare class, Tom Greenwald turned in this paper:

A Non-Paper on Lear and Tragedy

It would seem that understanding between people can only be accomplished through some act of tragedy, if accomplished at all. We are now living with an act of tragedy that defies understanding, and yet at the same time cries out for understanding. Tragedies are, sadly, nothing new to my generation. We seem to live in an age of violence and hate, where men of good will and good conscience are shot down in our cities' streets as though they were animals. Yet we as a people don't ever seem to learn the lesson. We never seem to do anything about it.

King Lear *is an excellent tragedy. Every student of literature should be acquainted with it. I, as an English major, can appreciate it. I can point to the generation gap and say, "See, that was a problem in Shakespeare's time, too." I can point to the disintegration of the family unit within the play and say, "That hasn't changed much either." I can feel the despair that Lear must have felt, old before his time, for he was not yet wise. I can feel the despair because I have grandparents who died without yet being wise, and I never took the time to try to understand them.*

Though I can appreciate and note these fine points of Lear's tragedy, something happens in Memphis or Dallas and I realize that I do not understand the why of tragedy. I can see how it happens, but I can never do anything to change it.

Friday morning standing in front of the Union, I wished I were black, so that at least my sadness and anger could be understood and felt by my own people. But my people do not understand; they do not feel. They allow the conditions to exist, they turn their backs. When something happens, they bring their dime store sympathy out of the closet and wear it on their sleeves for a day or a week, like a rumpled sweater they didn't know they had, and then they put it back in the closet, where the moths gradually eat even this garment away into nothingness, and they become even farther estranged from their fellow men. As the years go by, each generation hopes for change but the change never comes. People's emotions as well as their arteries harden with age, and they hide behind a wall of impenetrable insensitivity.

We could all learn so much from the tragedy of Memphis, but maybe genuine understanding only comes with death, as it did for King Lear. Until then, it will always be "we" and "they." "We" stand outside on the lawn and stare into the Union, and "they" stand inside the Union and stare out at the lawn, a people separated so much more than by just concrete and glass and chains. Were "we" standing in front of the Union in sympathy? No, "we" were, for the most part, indignant that "we" could not get our afternoon Coke. "They" had no business taking our Cokes away from us, that was too much. But next week it will make no difference, the Union will be open, and "we" will get our Cokes and sit where "we" always sit and "they" will get their Cokes and sit where "they" always sit, only "we" and "they" will be a little farther apart than before, where with just a little understanding the two races could have come a step closer to each other and could have been a step nearer becoming one people. But it won't happen, and it is "my" people and myself who must bear the awesome burden of guilt. Devils often have blue eyes.

Mr. Greenwald did not have to tell the other half of his story—how King Lear finally learned to see the "poor, naked wretches" who lived in his kingdom all his life. The other students in the class had just read the play. Some of them for the first time recognized King Lear's blindness in their own, which Mr. Greenwald had described so accurately.

DIG IT

In the local newspaper I read an article about a history teacher at the new community college conducting a "dig" with his students. Sounded as if he was taking the Third Way and I might learn from him.

Paul Millikan told me the whole story. At the end of each semester the students at Kalamazoo Valley Community College are given three weeks outside of the regular course for a project. He thought his students might dig for history and asked the director of the city museum if he knew of a likely spot. The director said he had kicked up a few relics, including an 1840 penny, near the supposed home site of the first settler in the county Bazel Harrison, who had lived to be 103. Mr. Millikan had just been reading a long document about the Harrison plantation on the James River in Virginia. That family included two presidents and a signer of the Declaration of Independence. Turned out that Bazel was related and had moved from Ohio to the Michigan prairies in 1827 or 1829 at the age of fifty-seven. He had been shown to his land by a Pottawatomie chief.

Mr. Millikan had his digging site. He notified five students he remembered had shown an interest in Egyptology, and issued an open invitation. Twenty students responded three weeks before the registration period. He asked them to buy a guide to field methods in archaeology and talked three days in class about the project and methods of digging.

Then out they went to a farm five miles away where the owner had agreed to let them work in a field he had decided to leave fallow that year. After a surveyor had fixed the position officially, they marked off two ditches at right angles to each other. The intersection point was fixed where an old settler had told the museum director he remembered seeing the log cabin as a boy. "Right off there from that great big dead tree," he said. And he was right. Soon they began to find artifacts. In the third week, near the end of their allotted time, they came upon the foundation of the chimney, and almost every shovelful revealed an artifact or piece of the building. Broken bowls of clay pipes, a flintlock, pennies as large as a quarter.

It was the beginning of a new discovery period. Although the school vacation of two weeks loomed ahead, many students wanted to continue work. They did. So much interest had been generated in the college and surrounding area by then that Mr. Millikan felt forced to form another class, made up of veterans and newcomers. The second group worked through the vacation period. The course was bursting the bonds of official calendar and curriculum.

The local paper ran two stories about the project, and one was picked up by a Detroit paper. Student diggers appeared on television four times. They decided that digging was too much fun to restrict to institutional limitations; so they formed a club, sat around for forty minutes arguing about what to call it and finally agreed on the name Diggers Interested in Recovering Traces of Yesteryear, the first letters of which spell DIRTY. They shortly called themselves the Dirty Society and planned to allow students who had graduated and wanted to remain dirty to belong to the club.

During these project classes, Mr. Millikan took his group on field trips. In Grand Rapids, the director of the museum showed artifacts from Hopewell Indian mounds and let the students see an archaeological laboratory. At the Oriental Institute of the University of Chicago, Mr. Millikan asked for a learned student guide and got him—a graduate student who walked around quickly translating the hieroglyphics and stunning his audience with his knowledge. He said he had never talked to a better group. The questions Mr. Millikan's students fired at him were based on experience. At the Field Museum Mr. Millikan told the students to look at exhibits which showed archaeological exploration and digging and to report back what they found. They themselves had been digging only into 1827, but the digs of ancient ruins spoke to them clearly.

As the students got themselves more fired up and improved their skills, they began to be called upon. The local museum director had other sites in mind. In a town forty miles away a citizen had set up a plan to dig and reconstruct a village consisting of buildings used in the period 1840-1890. Upon request, Mr. Millikan sent up two students to work there. They were given course credit for the project. A girl who was training to be a librarian was put to work cataloguing the papers of an early settler, and a boy interested in firearms cleaned, oiled, and assembled old guns and prepared a list of those manufactured in Michigan. In addition, the girl wrote a brochure that is being used to introduce the visiting public to the historical site. "It's one thing," said Mr. Millikan, "to write a scholarly treatise on something like this and another to prepare material that will make sense to a tourist who is spending only two minutes before a particular object."

Now this teacher can hardly keep his project within reasonable bounds. People from all over the area have become interested, and many want to dig. During the second session at Bazel Harrison's site, several elderly people in the area wanted to visit and recall their knowledge of Harrison's seventeen children. One day several old folks appeared on the site, Mr. Millikan said, "Go ahead," and they talked on for hours to students sitting cross legged in the mud, hooked on the American past.

NEW-S

Mr. Millikan's success came as no surprise to me. The principle by which he set up his class, like all good principles, was simple and endlessly productive. It kept manufacturing *new-s,* multifarious and exciting to students and teacher, almost every *new* in turn capable of creating more new-s.

The principle is to start right here (I am reminded of the aptness of the title for the magazine of student writing at Indiana State—*Here*) by encouraging the student to show himself at his strongest, in knowledge, language, habit, works produced in the investigation of something that counts for him because it lies in his here. And then to encourage him to study how other investigators, more experienced and professional than he, have carried out the same sort of task in a larger and more sophisticated way.

YUP

I had taken my eight-and-a-half-year-old son along to see Mr. Millikan. On the way back we stopped at a country store to buy a Popsicle on a hot July day. As we stood near the gas pump eating, I noticed in the window a facsimile of the Declaration of Independence.

"He said there was one of Bazel Harrison's relatives on this document," I said to Mike. We looked, and near the bottom found ***Benj[a] Harrison.***

"Yup," said Mike, willing to grant the fact, but unimpressed. I thought it was a great connection, but his response reminded me that the Third Way for one person is not always the Third Way for another.

THE DISCIPLINE OF HISTORY

In writing my Ph.D. thesis at Columbia University on objectivity and responsibility in newspaper reporting, I found out what practitioners in many fields think about the validity of their own investigative methods—medical doctors, botanists, historians, social scientists, psychologists, etc.

If I were teaching a history class in the university, I would begin by presenting my students with two accounts of one event, written by persons in my class.

For example:

1

I wish I had had my camera along at the Homecoming Parade today. Not to take pictures of any of the floats; they weren't that good, but some of the people were great. In front of the whole deal, four ROTC boys marched, high-stepping along, serious as hell about their solemn duty. The two boys on the outside had rifles slung impressively over their shoulders, the two on the inside were carrying flags. I'll never forget this one poor fellow with the blond hair and glasses carrying the American flag. The wind was whipping hard today and he was having trouble keeping the flag up. The pole was pressed against his stomach and his arms were straining. There was such fear in his eyes. I think had he dropped the flag the two boys on the outside would have halted and shot him, then marched on. The rest of the parade would have continued on down West Michigan, avoiding the body.

2

Today I watched the Homecoming parade. It was beautiful. The sun came out finally, and the floats went by all gaudy and temporary while the high school bands played. Some of my profs sneer at such displays. I can't see why. They're so glorious, so creative, so basic. Every human being in the world wants to experience beautiful people, bright colors, crashing music. A lot of people really enjoyed the day, and many of them did so without once mentioning school spirit or participation or whatever the catchword is now. People work together to create something beautiful and harmless and everyone complains. A parade is as much an expression of the human spirit as a museum or a cathedral. In fact, a parade is where real immortality is. If some man could find himself enshrined or glorified in a parade every year before and after his death, he would be immortal.

And then I could ask students to comment on the two writings. Soon they would be asking the essential questions of all history: What were the facts? What clues to the accuracy and validity of those facts stand in the accounts themselves? What are the attitudes of the writers toward their subject? How did those attitudes select facts? Does Writer One's large animosity toward the ROTC and war sharpen his perception as well as narrow it? Is the first report more historical than the second because it contains description of actualities? Should historians generalize? How? When? Where do the attitudes of the writers come from? Are they purely individual or influenced by the society in which they lived? Or both? And how much? Does history differ from journalism and personal opinion? Or does it encompass both and something more?

After such questions, the students would be ready to read Carlyle or Thucydides or Henry Steele Commager.

Letting the Slaves Talk

Halfway through the semester now in all my classes, I begin the two-hour session by saying, "What's on your mind today?" I let the students talk for five to thirty minutes. This week one day I couldn't stop them when they got on the subject of Sensitivity Training, which is an explosive subject right now in our community. I had thought I would have to explain the complexities of the matter to them, but a number of them had taken a course or a weekend seminar in Sensitivity Training, and soon they were pointing out to each other the dozens of methods employed under this name, and arguing the strengths and weaknesses and dangers of the technique.

Usually what they say in such free discussion relates directly to what we are doing in the class—whether it be Advanced Writing, or Shakespeare, or Criticism of Mass Media. That is no surprise to me now, because my students have taught me that the subject of all those classes is human behavior.

"I WONDER WHAT YOU THINK OF IT"

One day when I said, "What's on your mind?" the class fell into an extra long silence, as if caught by surprise. Miss Edick, who had frequently launched the class into a good discussion, started to speak, looked sad and confused, and then said in low voice, "*I don't know—this may sound awfully strange. Maybe I shouldn't ask, but I've had to think about death lately, and I just wonder what you think of it.*"

She looked around the room as if expecting instant wisdom and I thought, "My God, this will be a terrible session. What does she expect us to do with that question on the spur of the moment?"

There was another long pause. Miss Edick started to mumble apologies again. No one laughed at her. Then one student said she supposed we didn't worry as much about the fact of death for ourselves as what we should do when others lost someone close to them. Several agreed. I brought up the notion I had read recently in Walt Whitman, that before birth we are unconscious and not in pain at not being alive, but are a part of a universe preparing for us. He was hinting, I said, at what someone else had told me recently—that if we do not suffer before birth, we probably will not after death; and therefore the state of nothingness that is death is not to be feared.

Some students agreed. One said he felt unworried because he believed in an afterlife. He spoke without belligerence, and another student said calmly he did not believe in an afterlife and therefore did not worry about death.

At this point I was sure the class would choose up sides and the religious war would rage. But no. The students continued to put before each other their notions about death, and Miss Edick listened. Finally she said, "Thank you," and the discussion was over. From the first, the others had sensed her mood, serious and sad, and respected it. A week later she told me her father had been informed he had cancer and only three months to live.

Freedom as Religion

Today a young experimenting teacher I respect told me about his class in American Culture which meets once a week in the classroom and once in the homes of students or teacher. The evening talk sessions go on for three to five hours. Students bring their wives and husbands, and sometimes the teacher has to kick the students out in early morning hours.

"How do you handle the class?" I said.

"I just try to get the students to say something about themselves, what they believe, what they're doing. I don't bring up American Culture as such. It's them I'm interested in. Seeing how they approach a problem, how they connect their experiences."

As we talked on, I detected a disappointment. He said, "It doesn't always work. Last night we just didn't seem to go anywhere in the discussion."

His remark and my experiences with students recently made me realize why freedom and discipline often need to be separated from each other. In New English Shakespeare classes I have asked students to talk absolutely freely at the beginning of the hour and then later asked them to speak on a topic, like the character of Hamlet, which they have been reading and thinking about for some time. Often a day or a week later the class has remembered and used something said in the free-talk conversation. But in the second conversation, in which we focused on a topic that was a genuine part of the assigned work common to all, we naturally built upon what we had said the day before—always. That was our *course*, and we ran it together, had a notion of where we hoped to finish.

In the Third Way at the beginning of a semester—absolutely free writing in the writing course. But eventually work assigned, planned, focused—with freedom enough within each assignment to allow the student to find what counts for him. But discipline enough to insure that it usually also counts for the teacher. And if a student has found a subject choosing him alone, freedom to discuss it with the teacher and depart from the assignment.

But freedom as a religion, as a way of life, I have never seen work. Let's all sit down and say exactly what's on our minds and what we feel about each other—for thirty-six hours this weekend, or for an hour a day for six weeks. I grow tired. I want some habit, some regimen, some discipline to what I do.

WE ARE ALL IN CONSTANT MOTION

A girl who had been in my Shakespeare class signed up for Advanced Writing and turned in this paper about a speech class as her third free writing at the beginning of the term:

The course is designed to make us all up-loose. We sned our hang-ups and our role and become instantly honest people. Ten of us sitting in an apartment, naked of the selves we carry around every day. It's not honest. Chan sits in the corner explaining why he doesn't want to be the leader, but he was the first who spoke and he leans in, ready to take over.

Judy has logged ten years of group experience and I can see why. She never speaks. I wonder what's happening behind her short hair. She's not a college student, but she's trying. She's over thirty, and it's true, I don't trust her. She tries so hard to deny her age. If she'd accept it, so would I.

We have a well-rounded group. We even have a hippie. Ted sits cross-legged on the floor. Long dangling arms draped across his knees and picks fuzz from the rug with his bony fingers. His wire-frames hide his innocent long-lashed eyes. His long hair hides well the balding spots. I wish he would wash it so that it flowed and billowed instead of hanging heavy with grease. His chin quivers when he talks, and I wonder how many unwept sorrows he has.

Tom is tired of playing games with his head. He wants to live from his guts, but he's afraid to be angry. And is uncomfortable with sadness. I wonder if he's ever belly-laughed.

Chan announces that we will all love one another. I don't know. Maybe I'll hate everyone. After all, hate's just love turned inside out. Why do we need that guarantee anyway? Anger and sorrow are just as real as love and joy. They might be even more real. A wildly wet tear is more there than a dry calculated laugh.

We've been complaining of test-tube babies and date processing, but here we are, trying to recreate life with ten people in a too small living room. We analyze our behavior and others' so that we can find a system to file it away in.

Maybe next week we will be able to hang up our outside roles on the coat rack and resist the temptation to don yet another for the group. Then I won't expect Chan to be as he is today. If science is right, we are all in constant motion, so that categorization is impossible.

A CASUAL ACCOUNT

In my freshman writing course, one nineteen-year-old boy—I'll call him Dan Calmer—who had studied under John Bennett at Central High School, did not write enough. Often he missed class. I was disappointed for him because I had seen a powerful paper he had written in high school and knew what he could do. He just couldn't get going in college, he said; and I didn't inquire into the personal hang-ups he must be having. The few papers he completed were strong. One I took to the university president because it told some revealing facts about a country club the university had been having ideological differences with. Dan's account buttressed the president's position in the controversy.

At the end of the semester, after the last deadline for presenting papers, Dan turned in the longest one I had received all semester. Rushed with end-of-the-semester grading in all my courses, I took a quick look at the opening, saw the words, "No shit, she's a real pig!" and put the paper aside. I was tired of student writing that tried to shock me with nothing more than vulgar words. A day later I looked at the paper again and thought that if Dan had gone to the trouble to write such a long one, it must have some substance. I skimmed a few pages and saw it was a casual account of the student-police fracas cited on the first page of this book. The court had officially called it a *riot*. Dan's light tone offended me. So again I laid down the paper.

Just before the last class of the year, I took time to read all of it and found that its low-key narrative masked a real attitude toward the events. I wanted others to react to it. I brought it to class and read it aloud without divulging Dan's name. Here is an excerpt:

Their commander was in front of them giving them orders or something. The students didn't move. The cops were looking at each other as if to say the students were supposed to move when they assembled, what were they to do now? The commander got them settled down and barked orders to move forward. The street cleared in front of them and filled in back of them, a couple of slower students getting nudged around by the black stick . . . The cops came back down the other way and the same thing happened again. They made two more passes but the crowd still wouldn't break up.

On their last trip down, I spotted the girl in blue. She'd gone to her dorm to put a coat on. I nudged Dave and we made our way toward her.

"This your first riot?"

"Yeah."

"Me too. Exciting, isn't it?"

"Yeah, I wish I could see what's going on down there."

"Why don't we go a little closer?"

We moved toward the crowd in front of the buses. I heard a bullhorn go on: "This is (what's his face) commander of the Paw Paw post—"

Three guys right behind us responded in unison, "Fuck you!"

The commander continued. "Everyone here is guilty of a felony for unlawful assembly, and anyone we catch will be placed under arrest." This was met with the same old jeers and taunts and a brick. I stomped out my cigarette.

The hundred and twenty or so state police were joined by the twenty white-helmeted local police and spread into a single line that stretched from the student center to the president's house. On the whistle from the commander they started forward. Students scrambled. This time it was for keeps and you couldn't just move around to the other side of them. Everyone began running. I started my motorcycle. I cut across some grass to another parking lot. Cars were pulling out and taking off behind the dorms to Gilkison Street. Dave was walking right in front of me with that girl whose light blue slacks were moving nicely back and forth in front of us. . .

When I finished reading the story, several students said they liked it. No one complained about frank or vulgar language, and yet a number of girls in the room were conservative and delicate in their tastes. I looked around for demurrers. Everyone who was responding was shaking his head positively.

"*He puts you right there,*" said one girl. "*And all that stuff about looking at the girl in blue is very funny.*"

I then revealed the author by asking Dan if I had read his intentions correctly when I had written on the paper: "Gives me the feeling you're not excited about the events and at the same time the account puts down all the authorities because you seem bored and more interested in the pretty girl than in the main action."

"*Yeah*", said Dan, drawling his word and smile alike and finally arriving at that beatific expression of his that inevitably makes his listeners feel good.

A RESPONSE TO HIS OWN ENVIRONMENT

As I reflected on asking Dan to remove the vulgar words from his story, I wondered what he would answer. He might remember the statement of the university's aims in the catalog:

> . . . to develop in each student the ability to think objectively and critically so that he may be capable of assessing the validity of the information with which he is confronted and his own response to his environment. . .

THE READER'S HABITUAL RESPONSE

Once I comprehended Dan's paper, I began to learn from it. I wanted to use it in the review I had been asked to write on the computer report. But I feared the National Council of Teachers of English would not print the frank language in the journal *Research in the Teaching of English.* I considered asking Dan for permission to drop some of the words, but then I remembered an article in *College English* that had been haunting me since March 1967. I had written an appreciative note to its author, Lawrence W. Hyman of Brooklyn College, and yet here I was about to act contrary to his principles. He asked, "Why must intelligent and sensitive young men feel impelled to use such ugly words and describe such ugly feelings?" He said ". . . the immediate and prime function of literature is to make us see and feel the object or human situation in a way we have never done before." The novelist, he said, employs unusual sentence structure and diction "to break through the reader's habitual response." If we censor our students' work, said Mr. Hyman, "we are striking at the very function of literature itself."

I can see now that Dan and other students, particularly those writing for underground newspapers, are trying to let us older people know they are through with Engfish, the Establishment language. Yet much of their militant language offends me because it is overworked. It speaks like the schoolmarm who says, 'Damn!" at a party to impress the younger teachers, but in a tone that sounds as if she has asked for another helping of strawberry jam. I like my rough talkers to speak with authority. Shakespeare managed that, and Chaucer.

THEIR LOVE OF TRUTH

If I asked Dan to remove the words that were spoken at the police-student confrontation he was writing about, could I face these lines in *University Policies and the Faculty?*

> A superior teacher . . . conveys to the students the idea that he is their partner in the learning process. He arouses their intellectual curiosity, their love of truth, and their desire to know.

AT LEAST MORE FORMAL

For several years I have been reading newspaper accounts quoting students shouting "Pigs!" at police and have often thought how I would react if such an insult were hurled at me. As an Engfish teacher for many years, I had such an epithet coming to me. But reading Dan's paper, I suddenly noticed that the students were applying the word to different people—a college girl and the cops. I had forgotten that at least six years ago I had learned that men students call unattractive girls *pigs*. So now the tag does not seem so deeply insulting and violent when applied to policemen. The paper was instructing me with its truths.

These are not the times to meet students with new lies and hypocrisies. The authors of *The Analysis of Essays by Computer* wrote:

> Apostrophes are in a somewhat different category. While it is plainly more correct to write DON'T than DONT, it is somewhat better usage, or at least more formal usage, to write DO NOT. Frequent apostrophes might be supposed to mark a rather informal or casual style, and it might be supposed that informality is on the whole negatively regarded in a set theme assignment. On balance, therefore, apostrophes were predicted to correlate negatively with writing quality.

Percival speaking again. His comment enraged me when I realized that this decision, if carried out, would have prevented Dan from writing his case-history of the "riot." He could not have used contractions—"*When's that group getting here?*"—and his report would have had to limp along without verbatim dialogue. Dan is no dumbie. He knows what kind of weaseling is going on when professors say, "While it is plainly more correct . . . it is somewhat better . . . or at least *more formal*, to write DO NOT." He knows he is being told to write formally, damnit, even if formal is not necessarily better than informal. When teachers pile up a hundred, a thousand such hypocritical injunctions against telling truth, and then inform students that the university exists to practice and guard its sacred pursuit, I understand better why bombs are planted in the offices of ROTC commanders and deans of students. I do not want them placed anywhere on campus, but they more properly belong in professors' offices.

All Honorable Men

How could we teachers of the Humanities act like such monsters? I have said enough about the authors of *The Analysis of Essays by Computer*. They are liberal men. In the university we professors are all liberal men. And yet a few hours ago I was debating whether or not to print Dan Calmer's "Blue Girl," an account highly personal, highly factual, making a subtle point about the attitude of young Americans toward the Establishment. It is objective and subjective, tasting the smoke of a cigarette in the Snack Bar and cherry bomb in the street, recording youthful stirrings of sex (which are no different from adult stirrings of sex) and rebellion in authentic language.

Despite my recent regeneration as a teacher, I had not entirely shaken off my liberalism. I was about to censor Dan's account in the name of educational dignity and propriety. Yet a few weeks before that I had read in the paper that another account on the same subject—written with more skill and insight but still related to Dan's paper as father is to son, urgent in subject and frank in language (I am speaking of *The Armies of the Night* by Norman Mailer)—was awarded the Pulitzer Prize.

Evidence

Within my experience with Dan Calmer's case-history lies the core of what I have learned in the late years of my teaching career. It is that teachers must find ways of getting students to produce (in words, pictures, sounds, diagrams, objects, or landscapes) what students and teachers honestly admire. I believe I am not deluding myself about what happens in Third Way classes. No student does well all the time; but every student who carries out the program—respected and supported as an individual possessing the unique and complex experience that is every human being's lot on earth—moves other persons in delight or terror or sympathy at times. He is capable of seeing the world, human and natural, in a way valuable to others. And capable of learning from others to see it even more sharply.

Home

With the children in my family, in the relatively safe and familiar confines of my home, I find myself less capable of setting up situations which help young people grow and discipline themselves. If it were not for my recent success as a teacher, I think my failure as a father might lead me to a deep, unsettling despair. I can rationalize about that failure, saying that the children in my home and I know each other too well; we cannot move each other from success to success because the children know my failure to listen to them, or to apply the same standard to my acts as to theirs. And I know them, too, at their worst, in their pettiness with each other, their school-learned modish sadistic talk about the fat girl or the boy whose mother works at the township dump, their disheveling of a bathroom that is theirs alone. I can say that we see each other too much and live too closely, and that is one of the advantages possessed by a professor—he works under optimum conditions, seeing his students regularly but infrequently, and with the expectation (in the Third Way class, at least) that both he and they will ordinarily bring their best to the encounter. But I am still doing poorly as a father.

I am a better teacher than I once was; perhaps what I have learned about educating can teach me to be a better parent. Out of the corner of my eye these days I sometimes see the glimmer of a world transformed by millions of persons who expect great things from each other.

As the least drop of wine tinges the whole goblet, so the least particle of truth colors our whole life. It is never isolated, or simply added as treasure to our stock. When any real progress is made, we unlearn and learn anew what we thought we knew before.

Henry Thoreau, *Journal*,
December 31, 1837